What Board Members are Saying About *Board & Director Evaluations: Innovations for 21st Century Governance Committees*

MW00611672

"Beverly Behan's experience working with nearly 200 corporate boards has provided her with significant insight into how good boards can become great boards. Her answer: a comprehensive board evaluation process. This book skillfully discusses the process of designing and implementing an effective board evaluation and provides a comprehensive discussion of how to build a better board. It is a valuable resource for corporate directors and governance professionals." —**Nelson Peltz, Founder and CEO of Trian Fund Management, LP and Chair of the Board, The Wendy's Company**

"Bev Behan is an extremely experienced, knowledgeable, and no-nonsense consultant. Her latest book very much reflects her consulting style – offering practical, to the point, insightful, and actionable advice. Bev's expertise in board effectiveness clearly comes through in every chapter." —**Noel Spiegel, Lead Director, American Eagle Outfitters**

"Advice is always better when it's based on a wealth of experience – and that is what clearly comes out in Beverly's new book. As someone who has benefited both personally and corporately from her skills and expertise, I would highlight that board and director evaluations, when effectively designed, can be an indispensable tool in board-building. This book provides innovative ideas to help any board make the most of this exercise." —**David Sutherland, Chair of the Board, United States Steel Corporation**

"If you want a head's up on what the hot topics in corporate governance will be a few years from now, read what Beverly Behan is writing today. Her thinking is always at the leading edge of boardroom improvements and *Board & Director Evaluations* continues that trend." —**Ralph Ward, Publisher, Boardroom INSIDER**

"A true masterpiece on the topic of board evaluations from a global governance guru. Don't even attempt doing board/director evaluations until you have read this seminal work." —**Dr. Chris Bart, Founder, The Directors College of Canada and Chairman, Caribbean Institute of Directors & Caribbean Governance Training Institute**

"*Board and Director Evaluations* offers clear advice on designing a meaningful, truly effective evaluation process. It's a must read for Lead Directors, Board Chairs and Nom & Gov committee members. Beverly Behan has once again challenged us to make the boards we lead and serve on realize their fullest potential and set a tone of excellence at the top of the organizations we govern." —**Georgia Nelson, Director of Ball Corporation, Cummins Inc., Custom Truck One Source and Sims Limited**

"*Board and Director Evaluations* offers insightful thoughts and advice that even veteran Board Chairs and committee chairs could incorporate into their daily practices. Most practical of all are Behan's evaluation tools, which are useful to Boards of Directors for ongoing reflection and performance improvement." —**Milton Carroll, Chair of the Board, Health Care Service Corporation**

"This book hits it out of the ballpark. Easy to read, super insights and great suggestions for building a better board." —**Herb Wender, Chair of the Board, Radian Group, Inc.**

"Having chaired Nominating & Governance Committees of both private and public company boards, I highly recommend this book to other chairs seeking to get more value from their board and director evaluations. The author's 25 years of experience in working with boards in this area really shines through; she's written a clear, easy to read book filled with fresh ideas that can transform board and director evaluations from a 'box ticking exercise' to something that's genuinely worthwhile."—**Karen Kaplan, Chair & CEO, Hill Holliday Group**

"In today's world, a high functioning board is essential to a company's success. The important tasks of selecting the right CEO, engaging in the formulation and execution of the company's strategy, and overseeing the company's risk profile, to name a few, require a board that operates seamlessly. Board and director evaluations, when designed and conducted effectively, are critical for a board in meeting its key responsibilities. Bev's book is the go-to source for effective board and director evaluations: easy for any board to follow and implement. A must-read for directors and C-suite executives."—**Howell Estes, Chair of the Board, Maxar Technologies**

"Bev Behan has prepared a truly practical guide for chairs and members of governance committees. As a former member of seven commercial boards and chair of several governance committees, I found the book to be an easy read with plenty of helpful, real-world examples." —**Arthur D. Collins, Former Chair & CEO, Medtronic (NYSE)**

"As we embrace the merit of diverse boards, our paradigm has shifted somewhat in board composition decisions; potential and vertical strength are increasingly becoming the funnel through which new/diverse director candidates are considered. Many high potential candidates will have little prior boardroom experience and we, as Board Chairs and Nom/Gov Chairs, must champion the success of less experienced Directors. Beverly Behan's approach of interview-based evaluations offers a 'leg up' for today's new Directors and is something all boards should consider to make the most of their new board talent. And don't wait too long. Constructive Board Chair and peer feedback within 6–8 months should become the norm." —**John Cassaday, Chair of the Board, Manulife/John Hancock; Chair of Compensation and Leadership Development Committee, Sysco Corporation**

"I've personally worked with the author as a Director on two different boards, including one that undertook Board 2.0. This book mirrors her approach to working with clients – using board and director evaluations as a meaningful exercise that can significantly impact the board's effectiveness and create board alignment around some tough and important decisions. The best book on board and director evaluations you're likely to read." —**Linda J. Hall, PhD, Director or Former Director of 23 boards (public, private, and non-profit organizations).**

"This book is a refreshing departure from much governance literature in that it's easy to read, offers great ideas and practical advice that can transform any board or director evaluation from a rote, box-ticking exercise to something that's really useful in terms of board team-building." —**Muneer Satter, Former Senior Partner, Goldman Sachs Merchant Bank**

"Beverly Behan is not only one of the top advisors to CEOs and boards in the country, she is a brilliant writer on corporate governance. Her latest book is full of valuable insights and examples on best practices in board selection and evaluations. It's a pleasure to read." —**Kimberly Till, Former CEO, Harris Interactive (NASDAQ), Director, Catalina Marketing and Former Director of four companies**

BOARD

AND
DIRECTOR

EVALUATIONS

INNOVATIONS FOR 21ST CENTURY

GOVERNANCE COMMITTEES

BEVERLY A. BEHAN

Board Advisor, LLC – New York

ISBN 978-1-7347190-6-2 Paperback
ISBN 987-1-7347190-8-6 Hardcover
ISBN 978-1-7347190-5-5 eBook

Board Advisor, LLC
New York, New York
www.boardadvisor.net

To contact the author with any questions you may have relating to Board and Director Evaluations, speaking engagements (in person or by videoconference), bulk orders of the book and/or for any other inquiries relating to this book or the subject matter herein, please email: Beverly.behan@boardadvisor.net

Editor: Mary A. Metcalfe, M.S.

To My Wonderful Clients,

Some of the Smartest, Nicest,

Hardest-Working, and Most Impressive People

In the Corporate World

Thank You

For Giving Me the Privilege

Of Working with You

Contents

At a Glance............

BOARDS OF DIRECTORS are comprised of smart, sophisticated and accomplished businesspeople. Yet many boards waste their directors' time and talent when it comes to board and director evaluations.

If it's time to upgrade your board evaluation to something truly worthwhile – a process that respects your directors' insights, perspectives and good ideas – and engages them in an exercise that's not only enjoyable but genuinely impactful, this book will outline everything you need to know to redesign your board and director evaluation to something far better suited to the intelligent, successful people who serve on most Boards of Directors today.

All that's really needed is a boardroom champion – a leader genuinely committed to making their board the very best that it can be. If you are that champion, this book will help you to leverage some of the best tools available to make a good board genuinely great and to keep a great board vibrant. And your timing could not be better! Directors' newfound comfort with Zoom opens the door to using videoconferencing for board evaluations.

Beyond a comprehensive discussion of the key considerations in designing effective board and director evaluations, several innovations are introduced to further stimulate your thinking:

❖ **Building Board 2.0:** The best board succession planning tool I've ever used. Initially developed for boards undergoing major transitions (mergers, IPOs, significant change in business/strategy) it can be readily incorporated into a board evaluation.

❖ **Board Composition Benchmarking**: This technique uses the peer group created for executive compensation purposes to analyze board composition design. It can be a valuable, data-driven supplement to Board 2.0 or undertaken as a stand-alone project.

❖ **The New Director 360**: With both evaluative and developmental components, this process is designed for new directors who have been on the board 12–18 months. It reinforces strengths, nips problems in the bud and offers innovative suggestions for continued director development – a worthwhile consideration as the capstone to an effective Director Orientation Program, even for boards that don't conduct director evaluations on a regular basis.

Preface

The Role of Effective Board Evaluations in Building Great Boards

FOR THE PAST 25 years, I've had the privilege of working with the Boards of Directors of the S&P1500 and other public companies around the world. My job has been to find ways to make those boards not just good, but genuinely great.

The title of my last book reflects my personal belief: "*Great Companies Deserve Great Boards*" (Palgrave MacMillan, 2011). In fact, it could be argued that boards are more important today than ever before, given the pivotal role they will play in guiding the companies they govern through the economic aftermath of COVID-19 and other challenging issues now impacting the world economy.

Ten years ago, the hard-nosed Chief Financial Officer of a global company reflected on the changes his Board Chair had implemented two years earlier. These included the recruitment of four new directors, revamping the board pre-reading materials, prioritizing a fast-track CEO succession planning process and several other initiatives designed to respond to some fairly lackluster feedback on the way the board had been functioning. As a result, two years later the CFO told me, "Our board today – we get more value from them than we do from McKinsey!"

How was this accomplished? How do you take a board that's good – and make it truly great? How do you take a board that's great and retain its vibrancy over the years? The answer, believe it or not, is with a board evaluation. But not the kind you may be familiar with …

A board evaluation or board self-assessment (as it's sometimes called) for many years was synonymous with a mundane little process involving cookie-cutter survey forms that largely focused on compliance. But that's not the kind of board evaluation I'm talking about. If you're serious about creating a board that can step up to the challenges of 2021 and beyond, you need to tap into your board members' insights, perspectives and good ideas. Directors are among the most intelligent, sophisticated, and accomplished people in the corporate world. Isn't it time to treat them that way in your approach to board evaluation – and harness their insights and capabilities in creating a board that is not only good but truly outstanding?

I conduct board evaluations using in-depth conversations with each board member that cover all eight key parameters of board-building but are tailored to the company and its board, reflecting its ownership structure and stage of growth. I typically include discussions with senior executives who regularly work with the board, as well.

This format enables you to surface what the real issues are and get to the heart of them, more fully understand the board's current strengths and decide what steps you can take to make the board even better. Then you can move forward with those steps and start to reap the rewards of your work.

Why does this process yield results so quickly? Because of the way it's set up. By designing your board evaluation in this way, you'll have achieved three things:

➢ First, you'll have surfaced meaningful boardroom issues that can make a real difference once they are addressed. In my experience, the more effective the board is, the more engaged directors get – and the more good ideas they contribute through this process. Some of the best boards I've ever worked with routinely incorporate 8–10 items into their Action Plans.

➢ Second, because directors and executives have all invested time and energy to really think about the issues and offer constructive ideas about how to tackle them, you've created not only alignment around those issues, but a sense of ownership, as well. They're bought in! This creates a bias for action.

➢ Third, you've honored a sentiment that I've heard repeatedly in more than 20 years of working in the board-room: "Our board is unique!" And guess what? It probably is! That's why this approach works so well, whereas simply imposing the "governance best practice of the month" seldom does.

The truth is that every director wants to serve on a great board. Every Board Chair wants to lead a great board. Every Chief Executive Officer and senior team wants to work with a great board. What's often missing is a vehicle to shift a board from good to great and maintain a great board's vibrancy.

Over the past five years, there's been a groundswell of interest amongst Governance Committees – from recent IPOs to the top of the Fortune 500 – around the topic of board evaluation. Even Pricewaterhouse Coopers (PwC) pointed out in their 2020 survey of almost 700 public company directors across the United States: "Once, performance assessments may have been seen as check-the-box exercises. Today most boards take them seriously …"[1]

PWC's annual surveys in both 2019[2] and 2020 also found that 49% of directors believed that at least one of their fellow board members should be replaced[3] – and 21% thought that two or more needed to go.[4] The challenges presented by COVID-19 may have drawn these shortcomings into even sharper focus. This has been a time when companies have needed the best possible governance team at their board table; there may be less tolerance than ever for those not up to the task.

Once boards catch their breath in 2021 and 2022, they can do no better service to their shareholders and to the people whose livelihoods depend on the success of the company they oversee than to ramp up an effective board evaluation designed to:

---

1 PwC, "Turning Crisis Into Opportunity", *Annual Corporate Directors Survey*, (October 2020), 15. Accessed October 18, 2020, www.pwc.com/us/en/services/governance-insights-center/assets/pwc-2020-annual-corporate-directors-survey.pdf.

2 PwC, "The collegiality conundrum", *Annual Corporate Directors Survey*, (October 2019). Accessed October 20, 2020, https://www.pwc.com/us/en/services/governance-insights-center/assets/pwc-2019-annual-corporate-directors-survey-full-report-v2.pdf.pdf

3 PwC, "Turning Crisis Into Opportunity", 14.

4 Ibid, 14.

i. understand and recognize what the board's done well in helping the company navigate through the crisis and its aftermath; and,

ii. figure out what changes the board needs to make to be even stronger, better, and more effectively equipped to oversee the challenges to come.

But the only way to get after these and other critical board issues involves a shift from "check-the-box" board assessments to a more meaningful board evaluation process designed to gather actionable and constructive feedback through comprehensive, confidential interviews.

Interestingly, a new avenue has now opened for boards to consider– and its name is Zoom. During the COVID-19 outbreak, directors became both adept and comfortable with Zoom and its cousins in the videoconferencing world (Microsoft Teams, GoToMeeting, BlueJeans and the like). Using videoconferencing for board interviews may enable boards that have been on the fence about using an interview-based board evaluation to make this transition at last. Videoconference interviews can also serve to accelerate the board evaluation timeline and eliminate travel and other costs associated with in-person interviews. Throughout this book, I'll discuss ways of adapting best practices in board and director evaluations to facilitate the use of videoconferencing. I believe this represents a potential breakthrough in board evaluation design that boards today would be smart to leverage.

What to Expect from this Book

This book will outline a range of options to consider in refurbishing your board evaluation – and your individual director evaluation process as well, if you have one or are looking at implementing one.

At the outset, I'll talk about the kinds of outcomes boards can expect from a comprehensive board evaluation process so that you can decide if it's worth the effort: The first chapter covers some of the most common issues boards end up successfully addressing as a result of this process – and you'll quickly see that these are significant issues, not incremental ones.

Chapter Two will focus on the design of an effective board evaluation. I'll try to answer many of the questions that routinely arise in calls from Board Chairs and/or Governance Committee Chairs who are wrestling with a range of issues inherent in redesigning their board evaluations: whether they should use a third party, incorporate executive feedback, or include a board observation component. I'll introduce the concept of Board 2.0, an exercise that engages every member of the board and executive team in designing the optimal board composition of the future. This can be incorporated into a board evaluation or conducted on a stand-alone basis if a board is dealing with a major transitional issue such as a merger, IPO, or a dramatic change in its major line(s) of business.

The final chapter focuses on individual director evaluations. My experience with director peer reviews dates to 1996 and spans work since that time with dozens of boards all around the world. I've come to realize that the key to an effective director evaluation involves the ability to deliver feedback that is both specific and constructive. Here, I'll introduce another innovation, the New Director 360 – a concept recently developed from a project with a Fortune 100 board that wanted something more sophisticated for their high-powered new directors than anything they'd done before.

I hope this book will serve to answer many of your questions about board and director evaluations and help you determine whether and how to redesign your board's processes to make them even better than they are today – and truly worthy of the smart, successful people who serve on your Board of Directors. If you get your board evaluation right, I truly believe you'll get your board right – or at least, you'll make tremendous progress on that front.

In these challenging times,
we need the very best from our boards.

Chapter One

Typical Outcomes of an Effective Board Evaluation

BEFORE YOU GO to all the trouble of redesigning your board evaluation, it would be nice to get some idea of what you might achieve from those efforts, wouldn't it? So, before we dive in, let's start with this important question: What are the outcomes boards that follow the board evaluation process detailed in this book typically achieve? I'll try to answer that question by drawing upon my own board evaluation work with nearly 200 boards over the past two decades.

I. Changes in Board Composition

More than 75% of these board evaluations resulted in changes to the board's composition. This almost always involved a decision to recruit new board members (and typically more than one) with expertise/backgrounds most directors perceived as "gaps" in the board's current make-up. In nearly every case, the board either (i) wasn't actively recruiting at the time; or (ii) was looking for only one director and decided to expand the search to two (or more) in response to the board evaluation feedback. (For the record, I'm not a headhunter and had no interest in steering the boards I worked with in this direction; they came to these decisions entirely on their own.)

Only rarely did the board's size expand permanently as a result of adding these new directors. In most cases, the board chose to increase its size for a temporary period of 12–18 months while the new board members were being recruited and integrated onto the board. This strategy of "planned overlap" worked well for three reasons:

- First, it enabled the board to get on with filling the perceived gap(s) in board composition immediately, without having the search delayed and befuddled by the inevitable politics surrounding the thornier question of "Who's going to leave?"

- Second, it was clarified at the outset that someone would have to leave the board in 12–18 months' time to manage board size back down (even if there were no imminent retirements). This opened the door for one or more directors to offer their resignations and leave gracefully within that time frame – and it's what happened most of the time. Sometimes an informal discussion with the Board Chair or Chair of the Governance Committee during that interim 12–18 month period helped spur this decision; but the "planned overlap" strategy created the platform for this discussion to occur.

- Third, institutional memory is important. It's often overlooked in the quest to bring new directors with fresh perspectives and insights into the boardroom. A temporary period where new directors overlap and work together with all incumbents can have real benefits in smoothing the board transition.

Although rare, there were instances where a director offered their resignation in the board evaluation interview itself, acknowledging that they really weren't "the right fit" for this board. Typically (but not always) this occurred where the board evaluation process included either an Individual Director Evaluation component or a Board 2.0 exercise – both of which will be discussed in later chapters.

Beyond Age and Term Limits: Getting to the Heart of Board Composition Issues

Retirement ages and term limits can be helpful in spurring board refreshment. However, there are two significant board composition problems that age and term limits don't address:

(i) Director Performance: A wide range of director performance issues are, sadly, all too common in the corporate world. Some directors arrive at meetings unprepared and waste the board's time asking questions that were clearly covered in the board materials. Others dominate the board dialogue and weigh in on everything – often delving into minutiae or simply parroting comments that other board members have already made. More significant issues involve board members who treat fellow directors and executives in an acrimonious or disdainful fashion, breach boardroom confidentiality, or skate dangerously close to the wire on conflicts of interest. These shortcomings are seldom age- or term-related.

As will be discussed in Chapter Four, sometimes merely raising these issues with a director can make all the difference – especially when addressed with specific examples and advice as to what they need to do differently. I've personally seen dozens of examples of directors resolving a performance problem once it's presented in a constructive way as an outcome of a director evaluation process. Some annoying boardroom behaviors often involve fairly easy fixes.

Where the problem is more significant – and persists even after the director receives this kind of feedback – they have been put on notice. Moreover, the "notice" hasn't just come from the Board Chair or the Chair of the Governance Committee – it's emerged from a series of structured interviews with everyone on the board and is therefore much harder to ignore or dismiss as "personal bias." If a decision is eventually made not to re-nominate that director, the reason is now evident – and many board members in this situation choose to offer their resignation rather than face this outcome.

(ii) Background/Expertise Issues: This scenario involves a director whose expertise or background is the problem. Consequently, their contributions are somewhat marginal. While the board may have had high hopes when this director was initially recruited, over time it's become apparent that they are adding relatively little value – and many believe that this individual should be replaced.

Sometimes this scenario emerges when the company's business has dramatically changed; for example, the director with expertise in coal mining seems out of their depth ever since the company sold the coal division and invested in wind farms. Or the director joined the board five years ago when the company was a regional enterprise but struggles to make relevant contributions now that the business has expanded into significant international operations.

Other times, a board member's background is specialized and deep – an academic, a lawyer, a former government official; but this director provides only limited comments focused on a narrow range of issues squarely within their wheelhouse.

A different but related issue involves boards that have several directors with almost identical backgrounds – two retired Big Four audit firm partners, three investment bankers, or four mining company CEOs. Is this duplication of skills/expertise valuable? Or should one or more of these directors be replaced by a new board member who offers expertise currently lacking from the board's makeup that would be useful to add?

The expertise issue can be a far more insidious problem than director performance because it can't be fixed by behavioral changes or director training. As one Fortune 500 Board Chair explained, "You can teach people about governance; there are plenty of courses for that. But you can't change what they've spent 20 or 30 years doing in their executive careers."

The Board 2.0 exercise, described in Chapter Three, goes to the heart of this issue. Directors are asked to design the optimal board composition to oversee the company in three years' time. Skill gaps in the board's current composition immediately come to the fore. It also becomes evident that some of the expertise of directors now at the board table aren't on the list of "must have's" for Board 2.0.

This doesn't mean that the board needs to move from the status quo to Board 2.0 in one fell swoop. In most cases, this would result in significant disruption and immediate loss of valuable institutional memory. However, the Board 2.0 exercise sets up this transition to be accomplished thoughtfully and in a reasonable time frame. Most boards incorporate a first step towards achieving this into their Board Evaluation Action Plan, which typically involves director recruitment. Later phases (replacement of directors whose backgrounds are not included in Board 2.0) can be managed through the "planned overlap" scenario discussed earlier, at a pace that is entirely at the discretion of the Nominating Committee.

II. Improvements to Board Pre-Reading Materials

Roughly two-thirds of the board evaluations I've worked on identified board pre-reading materials as an area for improvement, which led to changes in this arena that significantly improved both board and committee meetings. Most boards have now migrated to digital platforms. However, this shift did not typically address "content issues" relative to the board materials. Whether board books are delivered to directors on a printed page or an iPad screen, garbage in is still garbage out – and the quality of board materials directly impacts board discussions and decision-making.

Busy executives often repurpose the materials created for presentations they made to the company's executive team. But a board-level audience is entirely different: unlike executives, directors meet intermittently with gaps (sometimes of several months) in between; a refresh and background on each agenda item is essential. Moreover, only a handful of board members are typically industry veterans. They're smart, accomplished businesspeople – so a "dumbing down" is inappropriate. But most lack the depth of familiarity with the industry, its players, its terminology, and its underlying issues that are almost second nature to company executives.

However, many of the issues with board pre-reading go even deeper: Far too many executives throw "everything but the kitchen sink" into their materials, leaving directors to wade through a morass of facts in search of the critical points and key issues. Perhaps ironically, many CEOs who complain about their board micro-managing need look no further than their board books to root out one of the underlying causes of this problem: Whether it's the Midwestern REIT that provided "move in/move out" data on every one of their two hundred apartment buildings, the North American restaurant chain that littered their board materials with the financials of each of their forty bistros, or the Asian conglomerate that incorporated multiple red-lines of modified corporate policies as a routine feature of their pre-reading packages – all of these companies took their boards "into the weeds" and then expressed dismay that the board "is always asking us about stupid little details that don't even matter!"

Even experienced executives often labor under the misconception that "bigger is better" when it comes to board books. Yet, nothing could be further from the truth. Quality, not quantity, is what matters. Research conducted in the UK by Board Intelligence and ICSA: The Governance Institute found: "The amount of time Board members can effectively read and digest board papers is about four hours per meeting, irrespective of the length of the board pack. The longer the board papers, the more that goes unread. And the greater the risk that directors may fail to spot a critical piece of information."[5]

Because board materials arise so frequently as an area for improvement in board evaluations, I often incorporate a review of the last two board agendas and associated pre-reading materials into the board evaluation. This gives me a flavor for both the format and content of the board packages: Are they always PowerPoint slides – including the executive summaries? Or in a "plain English" text format? Are they succinct or ponderous in nature? Do they stand alone? Or to they require a voice-over during the presentation to really make sense? Do they cross-reference the materials in the appendices? This review provides context for the feedback I'm hearing in the director interviews – and in some cases, problems with the board books are evident just from a read-through.

Where board materials – and management presentations – emerge as a key issue in a board evaluation, improvements typically start to be realized as early as the next board meeting. Changes are triggered merely by the board evaluation report – particularly if the report is shared with management. Boards that want to build even greater executive capability in this area might consider one or both of these approaches:

i. **Training Session for Executives to Optimize Their Effectiveness in Working with the Board:** Few corporate executives receive any training whatsoever on how to prepare effective board materials and presentations. They typically learn these skills from watching their boss and other members of the executive team, picking up both good and bad habits along the way. The most impactful training that can be developed for corporate executives in working their board uses feedback from their own board members as its foundation. In this way, a tailored program can be created that goes right to the heart of the real issues, rather than a generic workshop on presentation skills.

ii. **Individual Feedback on Board Materials/Presentations:** Several years ago, one of my clients asked me to undertake a somewhat unique exercise as part their CEO and executive succession planning process: I interviewed every board member to gather feedback about each of the five corporate executives who regularly presented to the board. The interviews covered their pre-reading materials, presentations in board meetings, and liaison role with board committees. My job was to probe for insightful feedback that the executives could both understand and utilize.

The results were illuminating: Complaints about the "crowded and confusing slides" that the Chief Operating Officer had been using in her presentations were traced back to a template given to her by the former General Counsel – and immediately discontinued. Another rising star discovered that board members had branded him "the steamroller" because that's how they felt in his presentations; he needed to learn how to actively listen in board meetings. The company's young General Counsel received accolades for the collaborative way he had worked with the board on some particularly thorny legal problems – feedback that reinforced his approach and meant a great deal to him

---

5 Chris Hodge, "The Hidden Cost of Board Meetings," *Board Intelligence* (May 17, 2018). Accessed September 28, 2020, https://www.boardintelligence.com/blog/the-hidden-cost-of-board-meetings.

personally. Not only did this exercise serve to enhance the effectiveness of every member of the executive team who received feedback; the changes they made enhanced the board's overall effectiveness.

III. CEO Succession Planning/Board Engagement in Corporate Strategy

"The big two" – strategy and CEO succession planning – emerged as areas for improvement in nearly three-quarters of the board evaluations I've worked on. Only rarely however, did **both** issues emerge at the same time; it was nearly always one or the other. From a practical standpoint, that's not surprising. A board's focus will often differ relative to the CEO's tenure:

- A board that prioritizes CEO succession planning typically has an incumbent CEO well into their tenure. Corporate strategy was likely hashed and out agreed upon some time back. While strategy is typically reviewed every year and progress against strategic execution constantly monitored, at this stage, the board is generally focused on planning for the company's impending leadership transition.

- A board that appointed a new CEO within the previous 24 months typically has little interest in CEO succession. Directors may reflect on their learnings from the succession process they've just been through, but their priority now is corporate strategy. After all, developing the company's strategy – and engaging with the board effectively on this pivotal issue – is one of a new CEO's most important responsibilities early in their tenure. Depending on the timing of the board evaluation, it may be that the CEO and board are gearing up for a major strategy process. Or the new CEO's first strategy offsite may have just been completed – perhaps in a way that board members found unsatisfactory. In either scenario, there is plenty of important board feedback to harness and leverage through a board evaluation.

a) Developing a Comprehensive CEO Succession Plan

Typical CEO Succession Issues that Emerge in a Board Evaluation

Where a company has an outstanding Chief Executive Officer, directors can be reluctant to even raise the issue of CEO succession planning. A 2018 Deloitte article captured the sentiment that often underlies this issue: "One of the CEOs we interviewed expressed the all too human instinct, 'Why would I want my board to discuss CEO succession planning? As soon as they do, my time here is short-lived.'"[6] But when the need to get a CEO succession plan underway emerges as a concern in the board evaluation, it provides directors with a graceful way to get started.

In other scenarios, a CEO succession plan is in place, but directors voice concerns about it: Some feel "in the dark" about CEO succession while others describe the succession plan as "pretty superficial". These types of comments often arise where the CEO succession plan has been developed by either the sitting CEO, the Chief HR Officer, the Board Chair or someone else – with limited, if any, input from the other directors. An ivory tower approach seldom works well when it comes to designing a process for what is arguably the single most important decision any board will make.

Over-reliance on executive search consultants has also emerged as a concern – and with increased frequency in recent years. A headhunter can be a critical resource in any CEO succession process, but it's important that CEO succession be driven by the board, with the *assistance* of an executive search professional – not the other way around.

---

6 Jeff Rosenthal, et al., "The holy grail of effective leadership succession planning: How to overcome the succession planning paradox," *Deloitte Insights*, (2018). Accessed September 28, 2020, www.boardintelligence.com/blog/the-hidden-cost-of-board-meetings.

Using the Board Evaluation Proactively:Gathering Input for the CEO Succession Plan

Where a company is 2–3 years away from their current CEO's retirement date, the board evaluation can be used proactively to collect feedback from directors and executives on a range of CEO succession planning issues. Three key components of a CEO succession plan that lend themselves particularly well to this sort of input are:

i. **CEO Criteria:** The establishment of specific, objective criteria for the company's next Chief Executive Officer is the cornerstone of any robust CEO succession plan. If the board has not yet developed criteria for the company's next CEO, board evaluation interviews provide a terrific opportunity to engage directors and top executives alike, around this important issue.

Criteria should reflect the company's business model, stage of growth, strategic direction, and corporate culture. It's important that the interviewer drive for specifics. Generic terms like "leadership" – which can mean something quite different to nearly everyone at the board table – are seldom helpful. What does "leadership" really mean to the person who used this term: Decisiveness? Persuasiveness? Vision? Prioritization is also critical – this means making some decisions about what's truly important and letting the other criteria slide. One Fortune 500 board struggling with their CEO succession plan had developed a list of 42 CEO criteria. This was tantamount to having no criteria at all.

Discussions around CEO criteria naturally lead to feedback about corporate culture – and some fascinating insights can emerge from these conversations. For example, the board of a manufacturing company didn't truly appreciate the headway their current CEO had made in fostering innovation until this became apparent from executive feedback gathered in the board evaluation. Interviewees gave examples of the CEO praising employees who had "the courage to try something different" and tolerating experiments that went awry, with the old adage "if you don't strike out a few times, you're not trying hard enough." Management underscored how important it was that the next CEO continue in this vein; they dreaded the thought of a new corporate leader who would "take the company backwards."

By contrast, the board of a biotech had suspicions about divisiveness in their corporate culture resulting from an acquisition that was never successfully integrated. The CEO was dismissive whenever board members expressed concerns around this issue, leaving directors wondering if they were valid or not. Feedback from board evaluation interviews conducted with members of the senior management team confirmed directors' suspicions – in fact, things were worse than they thought. Consequently, the board prioritized different competencies for the next CEO – a "unifier" was now considered even more important than a "strategist". The board also accelerated their timeline to change corporate leadership; the current CEO was gone in nine months – not the original two years outlined in the CEO succession plan.

ii. **CEO Succession Planning Roadmap:** This is a comprehensive document that outlines all the steps the board needs to take between now and an anticipated CEO transition date. The roadmap is an extremely useful device to help the board think through the various components of a robust CEO succession plan – and keep that plan on the rails, even though it should never be set in stone. Among other things, the roadmap should reflect board decisions around the following:

• Whether the board wishes to appoint their top candidate as Chief Operating Officer (or another role of institution-wide responsibility) prior to a final CEO decision. If so, when will the COO decision be made? How long will they serve as COO – six months, 12 months, two years? Will external candidates be considered for the COO role – or will it be a "final phase" in the grooming of the top internal candidate, with external candidates interviewed along with the COO prior to a final CEO decision?

- At what stage in the CEO succession planning process will an executive search firm be retained to assist in the identification of external CEO candidates? Will the board want a benchmarking study or "silent search" as a preliminary step prior to an external search?

- Will executive assessments be used as a component of the CEO succession plan? If so, when will these be conducted: early on with internal candidates so as to be factored into executive development plans? OR as a final due diligence phase prior to a CEO decision? Or both? Is the board comfortable having personnel from the search firm conduct **both** the external CEO candidate search **and** the executive assessments on both internal and external candidates? Or would they prefer to use an independent assessment professional in this regard?

- Plans for board members to get increased exposure to top internal candidates. This may involve having small teams of directors involved in site visits to top internal candidates' operations, having internal candidates play key roles at the board's next strategy offsite and other initiatives. When will these occur? How will they be structured? Who will take responsibility for organizing all of this?

Incorporating questions about these and other facets of the CEO succession plan into the board evaluation interviews can be extremely valuable, particularly at the outset of the succession planning process. Not only do board members tend to provide thoughtful perspectives on all these issues, taking the time to elicit their views creates board alignment around the CEO succession plan, which can be critical.

iii. **Internal/External Candidates:** An NYSE-listed financial services company asked all directors and six corporate executives participating in the board evaluation: (i) for their views on the CEO criteria; and (ii) to identify three internal and three external candidates that they considered a good fit with their CEO criteria – and why they saw each of these candidates as a "fit".

The responses were illuminating: One young executive who had never been considered a CEO candidate because of his age was repeatedly identified by fellow executives as having very strong potential to lead the company, particularly in view of his accomplishments in a key area targeted for strategic growth. The process also elicited over 10 names of very credible external candidates. Two years later, one of the external candidates on that list was eventually selected as the company's next CEO.

b) Designing a Process for Effective Board Engagement in Strategy

A comprehensive board evaluation can be a useful vehicle to test board alignment around corporate strategy: Does the board genuinely understand and fully support the corporate strategy? Are directors comfortable and conversant with key components of the strategy – and the "must-win battles" the company needs to focus on to implement it successfully? For CEOs and management teams who have done a good job engaging their boards around strategic issues, feedback that confirms directors' solid understanding and support for the strategic plan is gratifying – they often realize that the board has a more in-depth knowledge of the various nuances of the strategy than they initially believed.

In other cases – where either a lack of alignment or confusion around key elements of the strategy emerge during the board evaluation – this can be an alarm bell for management: They have work to do. However the CEO and executive team has engaged with the board on strategic issues up to now either hasn't been very effective, or the strategy needs to be revisited. In either case, surfacing these issues through a board evaluation is extremely important. They can then be addressed as one of the priority items in the Board Evaluation Action Plan.

As with CEO succession planning, a board evaluation can be deployed in advance of a board strategy retreat in a number of ways:

- The board of a regional bank in the northeastern US had recently appointed a new CEO, who joined the company from another bank in a different city. During the CEO recruitment process, directors complained that the prior CEO – who they'd terminated – had kept the board in the dark on numerous issues. They were happy with the collaborative approach the new CEO already appeared to be taking in working with the board. A board strategy offsite was scheduled about a month after the board evaluation. With this in mind, the new CEO asked to incorporate a series of questions relative to strategic issues into the board evaluation interviews. He felt this would give him a good sense of the board's take on some of the key components of strategic development prior to the offsite itself.

  The results were astonishing: Nearly half the board members failed to name two important new competitors in the region. Only a few were aware of regulatory changes that had the potential to impact the bank's operations in several important ways. And almost none had a grasp on significant changes in regional demographics – and hence, the bank's customer base. "Board members had told me that the prior CEO 'treated the board like mushrooms; he kept us in the dark and fed us a lot of '####'. Well, it turns out, they weren't kidding", the new CEO quipped. Learning about these "knowledge gaps" well in advance of the strategy offsite proved critical. A series of board materials were designed to address each of these issues and an attorney with expertise in banking regulations was invited to discuss the potential impact of the proposed changes at the board dinner scheduled for the eve of the offsite.

  The offsite ultimately proved a tremendous success: The board and management emerged fully aligned and excited about the bank's new strategic direction. However, the CEO was quick to point out that without the board evaluation alerting him to gaps in the board's understanding of critical issues "it would probably have been a disaster."

- The board of an industrial manufacturing company in the Midwest had been struggling with strategy issues for more than 18 months. Their new CEO, appointed two years earlier, had been lured away from a C-suite role at a much larger company and had never worked with a board before. His idea of board engagement in strategy involved lecturing the board in an almost academic fashion. If any directors challenged his assumptions or his proposals, he became defensive, even sarcastic. The board was not only unconvinced of the wisdom of the new CEO's strategic plan, they were shocked by some M&A proposals that emerged shortly thereafter, which many directors considered "completely off the wall". The problem was exacerbated by a somewhat volatile relationship that had developed between the new CEO and the Board Chair.

  The board had conducted a board evaluation survey with write-in comments about four months earlier, which were sent to the company's law firm for tabulation. The law firm reported back with low scores and a laundry list of nasty comments – creating a boardroom firestorm that only worsened the situation.

  A new approach – similar to the board evaluation process outlined in Chapter Two – was taken a few months later. Structured, confidential interviews with all directors and members of the senior executive team managed to unlock the real issues – and led to some productive solutions: The Chair received constructive feedback on a host of leadership issues, including some ideas to better navigate the working relationship with the CEO. A Strategy Committee was created, comprised of three board members: Two former CEOs plus a new director who had been a CFO. The Committee's mandate involved working with the CEO on strategy development to get the strategy in shape to take it back to the full board for further discussion. While Strategy Committees aren't always a solution to this sort of problem, in this instance, it served to leverage the talent of the board's best strategic thinkers and provide something of a "kitchen cabinet" for the new CEO, who clearly had reached an impasse with the Chair.

Interestingly, both these scenarios involved a board working on strategy development with a new CEO. Incorporating questions on key strategic issues into the board evaluation early in a CEO's tenure can provide tremendously important insights to any new CEO prior to engaging with his/her board on corporate strategy. It can also serve to establish the foundation for a highly collaborative working relationship between a new CEO and the Board of Directors. Strategy is an area where highly experienced board members can add significant value for management. Yet, many CEOs fail to leverage these capabilities effectively.

In Summary..........

The outcomes that typically emerge from the comprehensive board evaluation process described in this book address some of the most critical issues impacting the effectiveness of any Board of Directors – board composition, board information (which directly impacts the quality of board discussions and decision-making) and two of the most important facets of any board's work: CEO succession planning and corporate strategy. Other issues will emerge as well, often relating to board dynamics, the working relationship between the board and management and even issues around board leadership and board committees. Most evaluations result in Action Plans with 3–5 items that the board considers worthwhile; many high-achieving boards develop as many as 10. Every Action Plan is a bit different – just as no two boards are exactly alike. But whatever the final outcome, the point is this:

The issues you'll address as a result of this board evaluation process
will be meaningful and significant.

Chapter Two

Designing an Effective Board Evaluation

Champions and Preservationists

MANY PEOPLE ASK about the most important element in designing an effective board evaluation: Is it the questions asked? The format used to gather feedback? The report that summarizes the findings? Or the Action Plan developed as a final outcome of the process? All these factors are important. But the most essential component of an effective board evaluation is a champion.

A boardroom champion is someone who believes in excellence. They want to create and maintain a truly great board – and are in a board leadership position to make that happen. This champion might be the Board Chair or the Chair of the Governance Committee; they might also be the Chief Executive Officer.

But not all boards have champions. One of the most prominent shareholder activists in America once told me, "Do you know what the real difference is between the board of a private equity firm and the board of a public company? I'll tell you. When you're on the board of a private equity firm, much of your wealth and your family's future and security is directly impacted by the decisions that you're going make in that board meeting. So, you need to listen carefully, think critically, bring all your intellect and all your expertise to bear to make the best possible decisions you can, in order to increase the value of your investments. That's your job as a board member of a private equity firm. Do you know what the job is of a board member of a public company? To do everything possible to stay on the board."

While this remark was clearly facetious, it holds a kernel of truth for some directors even today: Despite all the changes boards have undergone since the demise of Enron twenty years ago, there are still some people who serve on boards largely for prestige and even for income. They're comfortable just the way things are – and they have a vested interest in keeping them that way; they'll do almost anything to ensure their continued tenure. Collegiality is their watchword – and their excuse for refusing to tackle issues of director performance, CEO incompetence, and strategic misfires.

Preservationist directors are far fewer in number than they used to be. Moreover, they ascend to Board Chair or Governance Chair roles less frequently because their boardroom peers recognize their lack of leadership and find ways to thwart their boardroom ambitions. But some of them do manage it.

Before you read any further, be honest about this issue: Do you have a boardroom champion as your Board Chair, Governance Committee Chair, or Chief Executive Officer? It doesn't have to be all three – but you need at least one champion among them. If all these people are largely preservationists, you should probably close this book right now. Because you're going to read about a lot of exciting tools and processes that can take your board from good to great – and you're going to get excited about that prospect.

However, if you don't have a boardroom champion, you won't get very far with these ideas. Preservationists often find them threatening; because they don't want excellence – they want to maintain the status quo. Boardroom mediocrity is just fine with them. In fact, it's pretty much perfect as far as they're concerned.

A boardroom champion, on the other hand, has entirely different goals and a very different vision for the board. They truly want the board to function at the top of its game and take pride in watching the board work together at its best. A boardroom champion values board meetings that are sometimes intense but generally vibrant, stimulating and occasionally fun – where the skills, talents, and deep expertise of those sitting at the board table are harnessed and channeled in a way that adds real value in board dialogue, debate, and decision-making.

Champions want their board to grapple with rather than hide from tough issues – to bring genuinely worthwhile perspectives, thoughtful challenges, and innovative thinking to the critical items facing the company they govern. They want executives to relish their time in the boardroom – and leave the meetings thinking, "Wow! Our board is awesome! They stretched my thinking and brought up issues I hadn't considered." Or, "That was a bit intense, but they looked at all sides of the question, challenged me, and ultimately gave me even greater confidence in my approach."

Simply saying, "I'm the Chairman of Company X" isn't enough for a boardroom champion if they know that the Board of X isn't functioning at the top of its game. Boardroom champions want to build a board that the other directors take genuine pride in being a part of, that company executives honestly respect, and that shareholders/investors would feel they are extremely well served by if they ever got close enough to see the board in action. Perhaps most importantly, boardroom champions treat their fellow directors with the respect that seasoned, accomplished businesspeople who are making a meaningful contribution deserve. As such, they resonate to the idea of a board evaluation that leverages directors' perspectives, insights and intelligence – and has real impact.

If you are a boardroom champion – or if you work with one who has asked you to consider how the board's annual evaluation might be more effective – then read on! Because the process outlined in this chapter will help you to build a board like the one I've just described.

Building a Board Evaluation for a Sophisticated Board

When you're working with a board comprised of smart, successful, and sophisticated directors – which we typically find in the S&P1500 and other public companies around the world – I find it helpful to think of board evaluations not as a report card, but as a platform for a terrific board discussion; a team-building exercise for all directors, which may incorporate feedback from the senior management team, as well. It should set up a robust and multi-dimensional conversation about the board and how it's working that all directors can get engaged around.

From that discussion, decisions can be made about where the board is adding significant value at present – and what changes could be implemented to make the board even more effective going forward. The components of the board evaluation process that I use and have refined over the past 25 years are summarized in Table 1.

Table 1: Comprehensive Board Evaluation Process

Steps	Description
Interview Protocol	✓ Should include all 8 key parameters of board effectiveness ✓ Preliminary discussions with Board Chair, Chair of Gov, CEO to ensure protocol is tailored and relevant; not "cookie cutter" ✓ Determine if corporate executives will also be interviewed – if so, a parallel interview protocol needs to be created
Interviews	✓ Zoom or other videoconferencing technology can now be used instead of in-person interviews
Summary Report	✓ Interview feedback is analyzed and summarized in a board evaluation report; typically 10+ pages in length ✓ Surfaces key themes including board strengths/contributions as well as opportunities for further improvement ✓ Actionable, specific and constructive – but protects confidentiality
Debrief/ Discussion	✓ Initial debrief with "sponsorship group" (typically Board Chair, Chair of Governance, CEO, GC/Corporate Secretary) ✓ Board evaluation discussion in working session with full board (60–90 minutes). Report distributed in pre-reading
Action Plan	✓ Action Plan created from the board evaluation discussion with the full board; summarizes the initiatives/action items the board has decided to undertake/initiate in response to the board evaluation feedback ✓ Describes how each action item will be addressed, where responsibility will lie to move the item forward, and a timeline

Interviews vs. Surveys

Board evaluations were introduced with the use of survey forms - and the majority of S&P1500 boards still this format today. Board surveys have been refined and improved over the past two decades. But my own preference for nearly 15 years has been to use structured interviews for board evaluations. Zoom opens the door for more boards to consider this approach.

A survey typically consists of a series of closed-ended questions which participants are asked to score on a 1–5 scale with some room for write-in comments. Survey feedback results in numeric reports that are often difficult to translate into meaningful action steps. Interviews, on the other hand, typically yield richer feedback and insights that get to the nub of the issue. Table 2 illustrates these differences:

Table 2: Surveys vs. Interviews

Survey-Based Board Evaluation Format	Interview-Based Board Evaluation Format
Topic: Board Pre-Reading Materials	**Topic: Board Pre-Reading Materials**
Question: Are you satisfied with the board pre-reading materials?	**Question: Could the board pre-reading materials could be improved in any way?**
Score: 2.7	
Write-In Comments:	**Interview Comments:**
<ul><li>"Improvement needed here"</li><li>"Materials are too lengthy"</li><li>"Not well organized"</li></ul>	<ul><li>"There are no executive summaries, and it takes me to page 30 before I really distill the key point. This wastes my time."</li><li>"There is a lot of industry jargon and acronyms in the pre-reading material. It's clear to me that management simply repurposes the materials they took into the executive committee and not tailoring them for a board level presentation."</li><li>"More use should be made of appendices for financial data. I want to see this data, but I would prefer five pages summarizing the key points; then let me refer to an appendix for more details if I want them."</li></ul>

Interviews are also far more engaging for participants, who typically enjoy taking the time (generally 45–60 minutes) to share their views about the board. Board members, by and large, are highly intelligent businesspeople who nearly always have good insights and terrific ideas on how to make a great board even better. The idea that directors are "too busy" to engage in this dialogue is nonsense; most board members welcome these conversations and sincerely appreciate the opportunity to provide thoughtful feedback about various facets of the board's operations.

Senior Management

Most Chief Executive Officers in the United States, Canada, the United Kingdom and many other countries serve as members of their governing boards and therefore routinely participate in the board evaluation process. Over the past decade, however, it has become increasingly popular to also gather feedback from top company executives who are not board members, but regularly attend board and committee meetings.

While some directors bristle at the thought of management "evaluating" the board, most find it illuminating to include management feedback in the board evaluation. Senior executives nearly always provide perspectives that complement those of directors and frequently surface new ideas that the board finds very worthwhile. This accounts for the expansion of the practice in recent years.

Including senior management also demonstrates the board's openness to feedback and nearly always earns kudos from the executive team. Moreover, it gives the board an opportunity to get management's insights on the "tone at the top" the board is perceived as setting – and its congruence with the corporate culture, a topic of frequent governance articles and even an NACD Blue Ribbon Commission Report in recent years.[7]

Typically, there are three to five executives who regularly attend board meetings, including the Chief Financial Officer and General Counsel. Regular attendees have enough exposure to the board so that they can provide excellent perspectives on a full range of issues being canvassed in the board evaluation. Including executives who only present to the board once or twice a year is debatable, as they may answer the board evaluation questions based on speculation rather than actual experience.

It almost goes without saying that if a decision is made to include senior management in the board evaluation, the process needs to be externally facilitated to ensure confidentiality and candor. No savvy corporate executive is going to tell the Board Chair – or any other director, for that matter – that the "tone at the top" set by the board is anything but glowing.

Yet it's vital for any board that truly wants to attain excellence to understand what the corporate executive team really thinks: Sometimes directors discover that the board is being "scapegoated" by the CEO for tough decisions – creating a fissure in the board/management relationship. Other times, board members come to realize that their habit of looking at unrelated items on their iPads during a board presentation has not gone unnoticed. And in many cases, the board is gratified by heartfelt commendations and genuine respect for tough decisions and important insights they brought to bear.

If senior executives are included, a decision will need to be made as to whether and how the board evaluation results will be shared with them. Some boards have no follow-up whatsoever with management; others invite those executives who provided feedback to attend some portions of the board meeting where the evaluation is discussed. It can be useful to postpone that decision until the board evaluation priorities emerge from an analysis of the feedback: If one of the major issues relates to CEO succession planning, for example, this discussion is probably best restricted

---

7 National Association of Corporate Directors, *Report of the NACD Blue Ribbon Commission on Culture as a Corporate Asset* (October 3, 2017). Accessed September 28, 2020, www.nacdonline.org/insights/publications.cfm?ItemNumber=48252.

to the board, itself. Enhancements to board pre-reading packages and improving the flow of presentations in board meetings, however, lend themselves particularly well to a joint board/ management discussion.

New Directors

Some boards exclude new directors from their board evaluation until they've served on the board for at least a year. However, I'm of the view that all directors – even relatively new recruits – should participate. A robust board evaluation serves as a team-building exercise for the board; leaving someone out defeats that purpose.

New directors are clearly not in a position to answer the same sort of questions as other members of the board due to their limited tenure. Instead, their feedback should focus on director recruitment and orientation – areas where they have the most recent experience and can provide particularly valuable insights. New directors can also be asked for their first impressions of the board's working dynamics, the board/management relationship – and might even suggest helpful practices from other boards they've served on or worked with.

Zoom/Videoconferencing

Videoconferencing neatly facilitates board evaluation interviews – and provides some distinct advantages over both in-person interviews and those conducted by phone. During the COVID-19 lockdowns, board members were forced to learn how to use Zoom and other videoconferencing platforms – GoToMeeting, BlueJeans, MicroSoft Teams, etc. Most directors have now become so comfortable with these vehicles that they don't just use them for business; they use them for personal chats with friends and family too.

Telephone interviews have significant drawbacks – chief among them, the inability to see the other person. When participants can look each other in the eye – even if it's on a screen – there's greater potential to build rapport and foster more open dialogue. A seasoned interviewer can immediately recognize from body language where there's something more to the participant's answer that needs to be explored with a few probing questions. The interviewee, on the other hand, can typically pick up on whether their point has been genuinely understood and intercede to offer clarifications.

As many board members live across the country – even around the world – in-person interviews have always been a challenge. Travel costs can be significant. Some boards schedule interviews with out-of-town directors around a board meeting – when the entire board is present at company headquarters. But this practice stretches out the evaluation across two board meetings (one to conduct the interviews, the second to debrief on the evaluation results). Squeezing the interviews between committee meetings is never optimal; when directors are in town for a board meeting, they are pre-occupied with the agenda items at hand. Videoconferencing does away with all these concerns.

The advantages of using Zoom for a board evaluation became immediately apparent in discussions with a global company based in the UK that had a new CEO. This board wanted to undertake "a more worthwhile and credible board evaluation than what we've done in the past." Their board members reside in Britain, Sweden, the United States and Singapore. Through the magic of Zoom, we were discussing a 6-week timeline – something that would never have been feasible with in-person interviews, not to mention the travel expenses involved. Suddenly, an interview-based board evaluation is genuinely workable for a global board – with far lower costs and an accelerated timeline.

External Facilitators

For more than 20 years, I've served as an external facilitator in conducting board evaluations for listed companies in North America and around the world. So, I'm the first to acknowledge my bias on this question. However, it's an issue that cannot be ignored when it comes to the design of an effective board evaluation – so I'll do my best to address it, as thoroughly and objectively as I can.

The 2018 *UK Corporate Governance Code* recommends that board evaluations of FTSE 350 companies be externally facilitated at least every three years.[8] This is clearly the direction board evaluations are heading, whether other countries adopt similar regulations or simply come to acknowledge this "best practice". In recent years, boards in the United States and other countries have demonstrated unprecedented levels of interest in working with an external facilitator on their board evaluation. Three of the main reasons are:

- **Candor, Confidentiality, and Credibility:** An experienced external facilitator can nearly always elicit more candid feedback than even the most well-respected Board Chair. This becomes even more important if senior management are included. Candor is fundamental to an effective board evaluation; if directors and executives aren't forthright and open in expressing their views, the entire process lacks credibility and has marginal value.

- **Experience Working with Other Boards:** Having someone facilitate the board evaluation process who's gone through this process with dozens of other boards can be extremely useful. An experienced external facilitator can offer practical insights on designing an effective process and avoiding common pitfalls. Moreover, when themes emerge from the board evaluation, itself, they can discuss approaches that other boards have used in tackling similar issues and the pros and cons of each.

- **Workload:** I once served as a resource for a Governance Chair who wanted to drive a comprehensive board evaluation personally. I helped him to design the interview protocol and debriefed with him after his discussions with directors, to summarize the feedback. When he finished his interviews, I conducted the analysis and wrote the board evaluation report for him. This process was a vast improvement over anything his board had done previously – and directors roundly applauded his efforts. However, even with this level of support, the Governance Chair found that the workload was far greater than he'd anticipated and vowed to have the interviews conducted externally next time, while he weighed in on key aspects of the process, reviewed the report, and co-facilitated the board discussion of the evaluation findings.

In choosing an external facilitator, it's essential to talk to references, particularly board-level references. Don't be surprised, however, if a seasoned board consultant refuses to provide references at an early stage of a consulting bake-off; most have Non-Disclosure Agreements. Moreover, their references typically consist of Board Chairs, other board members and/or CEOs whose permission is generally requested each time their contact information is given out.

Be wary of client lists, a popular marketing tool used by some professional services firms. Make sure to ask whether every name on that list is a client that the consultant(s) actually conducted board evaluation work for. One Governance Chair of a board in Montreal asked this question when presented with an impressive client list from a reputable North American search firm. When he did, the original list of more than 40 clients was reduced to eight; the firm had conducted search assignments, not board evaluations, for the other 32.

Once the board has narrowed its consideration to serious contenders, recent references should be furnished by finalists. In speaking to references, be sure to ask not only about their experience in working with the consultant but also about the impact of the work: What was achieved from the board evaluation? What kinds of issues did they end up tackling? How did this help the board to become even more effective? Don't hesitate to ask the consultant to provide

---

8 Financial Reporting Council, *The UK Corporate Governance Code* (July, 2018), 9. Accessed October 20, 2020, www.frc.org.uk/getattachment/88bd8c45-50ea-4841-95b0-d2f4f48069a2/2018-UK-Corporate-Governance-Code-FINAL.pdf.

a sample Action Plan from an actual board evaluation assignment (scrubbed of identifiers, of course) or for an excerpt of a board evaluation report. This gives you a sense of the kind of deliverables you can anticipate.

Frequency

Conducting an externally facilitated board evaluation every year is unnecessary. After all, a well-executed board evaluation should yield an Action Plan that may require 18–24 months to implement; repeating the process a year later typically delivers only marginal returns. As mentioned earlier, the 2018 *UK Corporate Governance Code* recommends external facilitation for FTSE 350 companies every three years, which is the model many boards in the US that use an external resource have naturally adopted.[9]

During the intervening years, they typically use a simple and internally conducted evaluation process that involves either a survey or phone call from the Board Chair or Corporate Secretary. This often follows up on the Action Plan from the earlier, more comprehensive process and may include questions such as: Are you satisfied with the board's progress in adopting the initiatives laid out in the Action Plan? Are these initiatives having a positive impact – or not? What else could be done in these areas?

Boards of NYSE-listed companies are obligated to conduct an annual board evaluation by regulation. However, the NYSE rules are silent in terms of the board evaluation process itself. As such, boards of NYSE companies have complete freedom to change their process – undertaking a very comprehensive evaluation one year and a more limited process the next two. Most other stock exchanges around the world, whether in a "comply or explain" jurisdiction (like the UK and Canada) or otherwise, provide similar flexibility. Even those countries that prescribe an annual board evaluation for their listed companies don't typically prescribe the methodology for conducting it. The Nasdaq doesn't even require its listed companies to conduct board evaluations – offering complete freedom in this regard.

Discovery Issues

In the early 2000s, when board evaluations were first required by the NYSE and adopted by many other boards as a "best practice", there was tremendous concern about the discoverability of board evaluations during litigation. This is a legitimate concern. From what I can see – and based on the views of many General Counsel I've worked with over the years – board evaluations are not protected or privileged and could be compelled during a lawsuit.

Some boards that were particularly fearful in this regard insisted that their board evaluations be "oral reports only, with nothing written down." Although popular in the mid-2000s, few boards that I know of have continued in this vein. Some boards chose to have their evaluations conducted by or sent to outside legal counsel, in the hopes that doing this would provide protection as either an "attorney work product" or through "attorney-client privilege". However, these sorts of privilege claims have never been upheld in a court of law. Holly Gregory, a partner at Sidley Austin LLP wrote the following in her fine article "Rethinking Board Evaluation" with respect to claiming attorney-client privilege for board evaluations:

> Using an attorney may preserve the ability to argue at a later date that attorney-client privilege attaches. However, this argument has not been tested, and boards and committees should not rely on this protection.[10]

The requirements to successfully claim solicitor-client privilege on a board evaluation may present a "high bar" when this argument finally does come before a court; board evaluations are not typically conducted in anticipation of

---

9 Ibid, 9.

10 Holly J. Gregory, "Rethinking Board Evaluation," *Practical Law: The Journal* (March, 2015), 30. Accessed September 24, 2020 at https://www.sidley.com/-/media/publications/march15_thegovernancecounselor.pdf.

litigation. That said, whenever I've had a client who wanted to retain me through their outside law firm, so as to preserve the ability to try to assert the privilege claim, I've been happy to structure my engagement in this way.

The issue of discoverability merits consideration at the outset of any board evaluation – even an internal one. And it should definitely be explored with any external facilitator you're thinking of working with. If this happens to be a law firm and their response to your concern is "solicitor-client privilege" I'd delve a little deeper, in view of the comments noted above. It's fair to ask what practical safeguards they plan to put in place in case the privilege claim doesn't hold water, if it's ever put to the test.

In terms of practical safeguards, there are probably more sophisticated techniques than my own practice, which hasn't changed much in 20 years. But this is what I do and it's a simple approach any board could adopt or insist upon: I hand-write all the interview notes; the paper notebooks are destroyed at the end of the project. Working drafts and the final board evaluation report are stored on a USB, not my hard drive. Rather than sending the first draft of the report to the Board Chair by email, I'll print it and send it by FedEx, if the client wishes – and many do.

With the Chair's permission, I'll print another copy and FedEx it to the General Counsel. Most GC's look at the report, tell me "It looks fine" and immediately post it in the "Board Only" section of their portal. However, if the GC has any discomfort, the final report is also sent to board members via FedEx. All paper copies are destroyed at the end of the meeting – and the USB is also destroyed at that time.

Interview Protocols

Using an interview format for a board evaluation requires an interview protocol to ensure consistency. Otherwise, every interview can cover a different range of issues, making it difficult to reach consensus on the findings. While most interview protocols end up being quite extensive, not every question is typically asked, though all topics are covered.

If senior executives are included in the board evaluation interviews, a slightly different but parallel protocol needs to be developed: It's nearly always useful to ask senior executives where they derive the most benefit from working with the board and to gather their views about corporate culture and the "tone at the top" they perceive the board as setting. On the other hand, questions about the CEO's annual performance evaluation, the director recruitment process, and other areas where senior management typically has little involvement can usually be eliminated.

There are three essentials when it comes to designing and effectively using a board interview protocol:

i. **It should cover all eight key parameters of board effectiveness.** These include: Board composition, board information/pre-reading materials, board agendas and meetings, board leadership, board committees, board dynamics, the working relationship between the board and management and board processes (which includes how the board engages on strategy, CEO succession planning, risk oversight, CEO evaluation, etc.). These are discussed in greater detail in Appendix A.

ii. **It should be tailored, not "cookie cutter".** The interview protocol should reflect the circumstances, key issues, and even ownership structure (if there is a majority shareholder or dual-class structure) of the board. This is what makes the entire exercise more relevant and resonant for participants. For example, if board composition/director recruitment is one of the most important issues the board is now grappling with, the protocol should drill down into this area and may even include a Board 2.0 exercise, as outlined in Chapter Three. If the board has just gone through a strategy process with the CEO and senior team that directors were disappointed in, the protocol may incorporate a number of questions to identify what the shortcomings were – and whether directors' unhappiness relates to the process that the CEO used to engage the board on strategic issues, or the strategy itself.

Part of that tailoring in 2021-2 should probably involve questions that gather board feedback on some of the tremendous challenges the board has had to deal with during COVID-19, board oversight around diversity and inclusion programs, and even the migration of board and committee meetings to videoconferencing formats:

❖ What are directors' most important learnings and insights from the risks and challenges the company faced during COVID-19? What did they feel the board did well in addressing those challenges and/or supporting the CEO and management through the crisis? What significant risks most concerned them in terms of the fallout of this situation (logistical issues, credit/banking/capital structure concerns, impact on major customers, employee issues, etc.)? Do they feel the board needs to strengthen its oversight in any of these areas – and if so, what would be helpful in this regard: For example, should this become a regular board agenda item in the near term? Should Key Performance Indicators (KPIs) be developed around this topic? What, if anything, should the board do differently if it finds itself coping with an unusually tough situation in the future?

❖ How well-informed do directors feel about diversity and inclusion policies and programs at the company? Do they have a good handle on whether these programs are having meaningful impact? What changes, if any, do they believe should be implemented in terms of board oversight of these issues: For example, should the board or a board committee be talking about diversity and inclusion issues as a more frequent agenda item? Should the board be getting different or better data relative to these issues than they received in the past? Is there value in creating a board/management task force on diversity and inclusion? Are there steps that should be addressed in this regard relative to the composition of the board, itself and if so, how should the Nominating Committee move forward?

❖ What have they seen as the challenges and upsides of migrating board and committee meetings to a videoconference format? What, in their view, has worked particularly well with the board meeting via videoconference? What have been the downsides? What could be done to make these meetings/videoconferences more effective going forward? Are there implications for the Board Chair in terms of how they conduct the meetings? Are there implications for management in their pre-reading materials and presentations when the board or committee meeting is held by videoconference? When the COVID-19 crisis subsides and the board can go back to meeting in person, would they recommend that some or all meetings continue to be conducted by videoconference – why?

iii. **It should be distributed in advance.** Once a draft interview protocol has been developed, it should be finalized with input from the Board Chair, Chair of the Governance Committee and Chief Executive Officer then distributed to all participants in advance of their interviews. Participants are asked to read the protocol over for 15 or 20 minutes sometime before their interview and think about the questions. This enables directors to frame their thoughts in advance and always makes better use of their time in the interview itself.

Directors often make some notes when reviewing the protocol. However, you want to avoid them having to fill out answers to the questions in advance. Generally, there's a "warning" on the protocol urging people not to waste time doing that. On rare occasions, a director will ignore this. I had this happen about a year ago; an elderly director who I think felt somewhat nervous about the board evaluation process, showed up with printed answers to every question and told me there was now no need for us to spend any time talking. I read over his responses quickly, asked him to sit down and got him talking anyway. Interestingly, the answers he gave in person differed – in some cases quite dramatically – from much of what he'd written down. He offered all kinds of important observations during our discussion that were not even mentioned in his written paper – and he enjoyed the conversation so much that we talked for more than hour.

Note: No sample Interview Protocols are included in the Appendices. If they were, some readers would be tempted to simply adopt them. Protocols *must* be tailored to every board to be truly effective.

Board Observation

When an external facilitator is used to conduct the board evaluation, some boards include a board observation component in the exercise. Attending all or part of a regular board meeting to observe the board at work can provide good context for some of the feedback being collected about board meetings, board dynamics, management presentations, and other issues. However, many boards who've tried this found certain directors "playing to the camera" – trying to influence the "evaluation" by suddenly become far more engaged than their peers had ever seen them as soon as the facilitator entered the boardroom. Others expressed concern that the external facilitator's presence tended to impede discussion on highly confidential and/or sensitive issues during the meeting. For these reasons, I seldom include board observations in my evaluation design. However, there may be instances in which it seems appropriate to do so – and it's something to think about.

With many board meetings now migrating to a videoconferencing format, inclusion of a board observation component has perhaps never been easier. However, this also creates some risk that the observation exercise may end up focusing on technical issues with the videoconferencing platform.

Whether the observation is planned for an in-person board meeting or a videoconference, one important consideration is timing: adding an observation component to the board evaluation inevitably expands the evaluation timeline – as one board meeting is required for the observation exercise and a second for the board discussion of the evaluation results. This may or may not be a significant issue depending on the frequency of board meetings.

Debrief and Action Planning

A great deal of thought typically goes into the feedback collection mechanism for the board evaluation. Less attention is often paid to what may be an even more important consideration: how to use the results of the board evaluation productively.

Interview-based board evaluations typically yield rich and constructive feedback that lends itself to good discussion. They also provide a level of specificity that enables the board to readily understand the crux of any issues surfaced and make some decisions as to whether and how to address them. At least 3–5 potential opportunities for further board enhancement should emerge from the board evaluation process; boards with highly engaged and very thoughtful directors often have 8–10.

Once the feedback is collected and analyzed, a report summarizing the results of the board evaluation is developed, which is generally reviewed at the outset by board leadership: The Board Chair, the Chair of the Governance Committee, and then with the Chief Executive Officer. This review enables a determination to be made of those issues worthy of discussion at a meeting of the full board and/or the Governance Committee – and how much time should be allocated on the board agenda for this working session to discuss the board evaluation results. As mentioned earlier, the General Counsel or Corporate Secretary are frequently included in this preliminary review as well, although generally the report is shared with them after board and corporate leadership have seen it.

The length of time required for the board's discussion of the evaluation can vary: some boards prefer to have the more in-depth discussion at the Governance Committee, scheduling the committee meeting for 1–2 hours and limiting the discussion by the full board to about half an hour. Most, however, prefer to give the full board an opportunity to discuss the board evaluation in depth, which typically requires 60–90 minutes on the board agenda, depending on the number of issues surfaced from the evaluation that board leadership decides to address during this session.

Distributing the board evaluation report to all directors in the pre-reading material makes the best use of the board's time in this meeting, as all directors will have read the report and come into the meeting prepared to discuss priority issues. Goals of this working session with the full board to discuss the board evaluation are generally threefold:

1. To have a good, interactive dialogue of the issues surfaced from the board evaluation that may yield worthwhile opportunities for constructive changes.

2. To explore alternative approaches to address the issues, including, as appropriate, tactics that other boards have adopted to address similar issues.

3. To reach decisions as to the best way to approach each issue, if at all.

At the conclusion, an Action Plan is created to capture key decisions from the meeting, which the board can use as a roadmap over the next 12–18 months in moving forward with these initiatives. Samples of Board Evaluation Action Plans are provided in Appendices B-1 and B-2.

In Summary..........

This chapter describes various elements for the board to consider in designing an effective board evaluation process for a sophisticated board:

*   the use of structured, confidential interviews,

*   incorporating senior management's perspectives,

*   developing tailored protocols that ensure consistency while recognizing the unique circumstances and issues of every board and practical ideas to offset discoverability concerns.

Directors' newfound comfort with Zoom opens the door to using videoconferencing to introduce interview-based board evaluations, changing the entire complexion of the board evaluation process to a platform for worthwhile discussion about genuinely important issues in board-building that leads to meaningful and continuous improvement.

However, the most essential element in the design of an effective board evaluation is a boardroom champion – a leader committed to genuine boardroom excellence who unleashes directors' insights, perspectives, and good ideas in service of this important goal.

Chapter Three

Building Board 2.0

ROUGHLY 75% OF the board evaluations I've been involved in over the past two decades resulted in changes to board composition. It was easy to get traction around this issue once you stopped having directors circle 1–5 on a survey form in response to closed-ended questions like "Our board composition is appropriate" and instead asked this simple question in an interview: "If the board were going to add one new director right now, what skills, expertise, or background would you prioritize in a new board colleague?"

Of course, you nearly always had to probe a bit to generate the kind of specific feedback that's actually useful. For example, if someone said, "We need more financial expertise," what do they really have in mind? A Chief Financial Officer, a retired Big Four audit partner, an investment banker or private equity partner? Why are they of this opinion? Is it because the company is doing more merger and acquisition (M&A) transactions? Or because the person everybody thought would succeed the current Audit Committee Chair hasn't been carrying their weight?

Three times out of four, there was clear consensus that a particular background was missing – and good reasons to prioritize it. This, of course, begged the question: "Should we wait until one of the board members hits the board retirement age before we fill that gap? Or should we find a new director right away with the expertise we need – even if the board size expands temporarily?" Not all boards chose to address a composition "gap" immediately. But the vast majority did, particularly when there was clear board consensus on what was missing and why it was important.

It wasn't always a functional skill set that was seen as a "gap"– such as an industry background, global/international experience or digital technology expertise. Sometimes it was a concern about diversity – and age diversity was often a factor, not only gender and ethnicity. Sometimes it was a desire to recruit one or two directors with Chair potential (as no one on the board was viewed as a successor to the current Chair and the board wanted to "get out ahead" of that issue before the Chair's retirement loomed). Geography occasionally entered the mix: if the entire board was from the Pacific Northwest, bringing on a few directors from other parts of the country became an important consideration if a national expansion was underway.

Board composition is the *single most important* of the eight key parameters of board-building outlined in Appendix A. Putting together an impressive team of directors is no guarantee that the board itself, will be effective. Unless the other seven parameters are also addressed, even a well-composed board with outstanding directors is generally sub-optimized and its tremendous potential wasted. However, pulling all the other seven levers of board effectiveness will achieve only marginal results if the board has the wrong make-up to begin with. This is why board composition is such a critical factor in creating a high-performing board.

The Genesis of Board 2.0

The Board 2.0 concept originated during a client project where three boards were merging into one. Politics were running rampant around the thorny issue of who would stay and who would go in the creation of the new Board of Directors to oversee the merged entity – referred to as Board 2.0. We wanted to cut through the politics by having some objective and practical criteria for director selection. Most importantly, we wanted to create a truly outstanding board – with the right mix of skills and expertise to add real value in overseeing the merged company.

Many boards at that time were using a Board Skills Matrix. But for various reasons, we didn't think this approach would achieve our aims. It seemed a bit "ivory tower" – somebody would go away and create the Skills Matrix, then try to persuade everyone else of its merits. With the current board politics, this approach was not going to get much traction. A Skills Matrix typically creates only general categories. It also frequently conflates background/expertise (which probably should be a bit different for every board seat) and personal qualities/characteristics (which all board members should have).

So, we decided to take a different tact – one that engaged all board members and executives, forced prioritization, and focused on optimizing the mix of expertise on Board 2.0. I met with every director serving on each of the three boards, as well as with the CEO who would lead the merged company and several members of the executive team. Using Graphic 1, I told each interviewee to assume: (i) that Board 2.0 would consist of 10 directors; (ii) that one board seat would be allocated to the CEO, leaving nine for independent directors, one of whom would serve as Board Chair, consistent with current practice.

Then, I asked each respondent what skills, experience and/or background they'd want to have in each of these nine board seats to create the best possible board to oversee the merged company. I didn't want names; this wasn't a vote on who should remain at the board table and who should leave. It was an effort to define the optimal skills and experience to effectively govern the new company.

Graphic 1: Board 2.0 Template

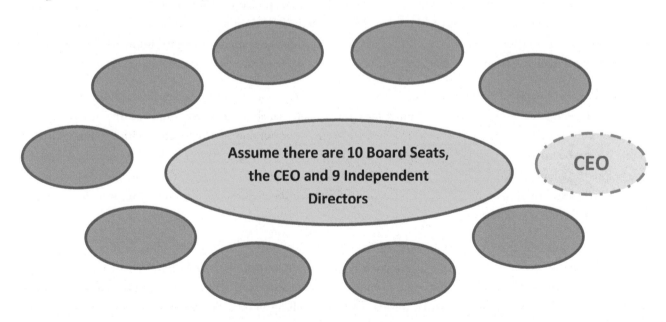

Assume there are 10 Board Seats, the CEO and 9 Independent Directors

CEO

In working through the Board 2.0 exercise with each interviewee, I found that I needed to do two things:

i. **Keep the respondent from giving too much consideration to the people already sitting on the three predecessor boards**. I wanted them focused only on the best possible board composition for Board 2.0 in terms of skills/expertise, given the merged company's business model and likely strategic direction. Sometimes, this resulted in recommendations of backgrounds not currently found among any of the directors on the three predecessor boards.

ii. **Probe to avoid generalities.** Only in this way could we arrive at a workable level of specificity that could be used in making decisions about who should be on the new board. I also wanted to understand the reasoning behind the expertise each interviewee was recommending: How did this suggested background relate to issues that Board 2.0 would be grappling with?

For example, if the respondent said, "I'd certainly want two or three people with experience in our industry," I'd ask how they define the "industry". Some respondents had a narrow definition (e.g., medical insurance); others saw this question more broadly (e.g., "anything in healthcare, actually I like the idea of a hospital CEO" or "anything in the insurance industry, even life or property/casualty insurance"). I'd ask what sort of job within the industry the individual should have held: A CEO or COO? A senior staff position, such as finance or regulatory affairs? Or a Chief Medical Officer? What were the reasons for these recommendations?

It was important to use a finite number of board seats. This forced interviewees to prioritize how best to "spend" each of the nine available seats. We also discussed criteria for the Board Chair.

These conversations were terrific. Every interviewee offered well-considered answers. And every Board 2.0 chart was different in some way. Out of more than 35 interviews, no two charts were the same!

But it didn't take long from studying these charts for the optimal make-up of Board 2.0 to emerge. Of the nine independent director seats, there was strong alignment with respect to the background/expertise that should be in six of them. As for the others, there were several pockets of agreement and some interesting "one of" ideas that gained a lot of traction when they were discussed. In the end, it was not difficult for all three boards to reach consensus on the final design for Board 2.0.

Although 22 former directors found themselves without a seat at the new board table, it was relatively harmonious. Everyone had been given an opportunity to express their views on what Board 2.0 should look like – and the choices about 'who would stay' as a member of Board 2.0 reflected the board composition derived from this exercise. Two new directors were also recruited – something that would have met with tremendous opposition without the Board 2.0 exercise. With it, there was a clear understanding and acceptance of the fact that these recruitments were necessary: The two new directors brought expertise that was considered essential in the composition of Board 2.0; no one on any of the three predecessor boards had it.

As it turned out, there were several women and people of color from the three predecessor boards who fit the criteria for seats on Board 2.0; this factor enabled Board 2.0 to seamlessly achieve its diversity objectives. A set of Board Expectations was also created, as discussed in Chapter Four.

The Board 2.0 exercise worked so well that I began adapting it to other client scenarios where boards were undergoing major transitions:

> *Significant Change in Business/Strategy:* The company had sold its largest division and used the proceeds to make an acquisition in a new line of business, somewhat adjacent to but dramatically different from its

core business for 20+ years. The acquisition was already generating nearly half the company's revenues and expected to grow significantly. In short, this company was dramatically transitioning its business, but had yet to transition its board to reflect these changes.

➤ ***High Level of Board Turnover Occasioned by Retirement:*** Four directors (one-third of the board) were all scheduled to reach the board's mandatory retirement age within two years' time. The company also had a new CEO who wanted to derive more value from the board. He was concerned that the Governance Committee seemed overly focused on replacing the expertise that would be lost through the upcoming retirements. Before any director recruitment began, he wanted to reconsider the board's entire composition and reach agreement on what the board should look like in three years' time.

➤ ***Initial Public Offering Scenarios:*** One IPO involved the spin-off of a major division of a Fortune 500 company. Another involved a company that had held its initial public offering (IPO) 18 months earlier; now, private equity investors were selling down their positions and the time had come to replace their seats at the board table. Both involved wholesale board composition design.

Board 2.0 was extremely useful in all these scenarios. Thereafter, I began incorporating it into some board evaluations where there were no major transition events. It's easy to include Board 2.0 as a component of an interview-based board evaluation, even when the interview is conducted on Zoom or another videoconferencing platform, so long as it enables screen sharing. However, Board 2.0 does not lend itself well to a survey format, as there is no opportunity to probe for specificity or the rationale behind the various Board 2.0 recommendations; both are essential for the exercise to be effective.

Optimal Board Size

I've seen boards of seven directors operate extremely effectively. And I've seen a board of 13 – which most would describe as "far too big" – hit it out of the park because they had an outstanding Chair who facilitated great meetings and a mix of skills and expertise that brought insightful and varied perspectives into the board discussions. Frankly, any board size within that range can probably work. I think it's a mistake to be overly prescriptive about the size of the board. Far too often, the mantra of maintaining board size is used as an excuse to defer adding much-needed expertise – a favorite entrenchment device of board preservationists.

Optimal Board Composition

Optimal board composition is different for every board. And, it is always a work in progress. It varies with the company's business model, stage of growth, ownership structure, and corporate strategy. What distinguishes a well-composed board is the evident nexus between the backgrounds of board members and the company's business.

The real job of a Nominating Committee isn't to recruit, nominate and re-nominate directors – as their committee charters almost uniformly state. The real job of a Nominating Committee is to put the best possible team of directors around the board table to govern the company effectively – people with the expertise to throw down the gauntlet to management, raise "red flags" and inject useful perspectives on critical corporate issues. It's readily apparent from looking at any board's composition whether the committee has been largely fulfilling this key responsibility – or falling woefully short.

When you look at director profiles on a company's website or annual proxy circular, you should be nodding your head as you read those bios thinking, "Yes, it makes a lot of sense to have someone with that background on this board." You shouldn't be scratching your head, puzzled as to how this individual's experience seems relevant and wondering how they could possibly make worthwhile contributions in overseeing this company.

Every board's makeup will and should differ, to reflect the company's business and strategy. That said, the boards of most public companies typically include:

> **Finance expertise** – All US boards need at least one director who qualifies as a Sarbanes-Oxley[11] financial expert on their Audit Committee; most other countries have similar regulatory requirements. Many boards, however, have two or three directors with strong financial acumen. Retired Big Four partners were prioritized in the mid-2000s. Over the past decade, a Chief Financial Officer background has become increasingly popular; some boards feel that CFOs have more breadth, as they can oversee the audit process and offer expertise on capital finance and M&A transactions. Many also choose to recruit finance experts with entirely different backgrounds, such as investment banking, commercial banking, or private equity.

> **Operational experience at a company of similar size/scope/complexity** – It's critical for any board to include at least a few directors who have served in an operating role (Profit and Loss (P&L) vs. staff responsibilities). Boards deal with such a wide range of issues – from corporate strategy to executive compensation to M&A transactions – that it makes good sense to have some directors at the board table who have faced a breadth of executive decisions. A Chief Executive Officer or Chief Operating Officer is the background most boards look for in this regard; however, some believe that an executive who ran a major business unit can also fit the bill. Occasionally, a board is lucky enough to recruit a director that combines operational and industry experience.

Whether from within or outside the industry, the key factor here is that director's experience should involve a senior operational role at a company or business unit similar in size, scope, and complexity to the one they'll be governing. For example, a global company will probably insist that at least a few people at their board table will have run a comparable international business, rather than businesses that may even be larger in size, but national in scope. Interestingly, a spin-off from a Fortune 500 rejected the idea of having a lot of Fortune 500 executives on its IPO board: "Once we are independent, we become a mid-cap. We will have far different issues and more limited resources than our parent. For this reason, we need directors who understand mid-cap issues – not people who have spent their whole careers in big Fortune 500 companies."

> **Industry experience** – The most recent PwC Directors Survey found a drop in the percentage of directors who considered industry experience "very important" from 70% to 43%.[12] Nonetheless, many boards consider it essential to have one or two independent directors at the board table who have worked in the company's industry. In fact, a board without any directors with an industry background has been viewed as a "red flag" by some investors.[13] Industry veterans can often challenge management more adeptly than any other members of the board simply because they know the business so well. This is also the reason many CEOs routinely describe board members with an industry background as adding the greatest value for them and for their management team.

The definition of the "industry", however, often requires some debate: For a silver mining company, for example, does "industry experience" consist of experience in "silver" or "metals" or "mining"? Industry veterans generally need to be retired or working in another industry to avoid conflicts of interest. Some boards

---

11 In 2003, the SEC adopted rules implementing section 407 of the Sarbanes-Oxley Act of 2002 (SOX), requiring a public company to disclose whether at least one audit committee financial expert (ACFE) serves on its audit committee or to disclose the reason for not having such an expert. Source: *The CPA Journal*. Accessed October 20, 2020, www.cpajournal.com/2016/06/12/sec-audit-committee-financial-expert/

12 PwC, "Turning crisis into opportunity", 13.

13 Ronald O'Hanley and Rakhi Kuman, "Changing Board Practices and Culture to Meet Investor Expectations," *IQ Insights* (State Street Global Advisors, August, 2016). Accessed September 29, 2020, https://www.faegredrinker.com/webfiles/5%20State%20Street%20Insights%20on%20Changing%20Board%20Practices.pdf.

have overcome this issue by recruiting from other geographies – an approach that has become increasingly difficult to navigate in a global economy.

➢ **Technology expertise** – This is a background many boards have prioritized over the past decade. Its importance often varies by industry: technology expertise is considered essential in retail, for example, but may be less of a priority for a mining company. But even boards that prioritize "technology" often lack alignment around what sort of tech background they really want: Is this a Chief Information Officer? A cybersecurity specialist? A digital marketing or eCommerce expert? Or the CEO of a Silicon Valley company that operates around the world?

As the backgrounds of 'technology experts' can be so varied, it's important to carefully consider these sorts of questions: Is this someone who can call B.S. on a technology presentation and/or challenge the company's progress in bringing in a major tech project on time and within budget? Or is this someone who can weigh in knowledgeably on critical issues around social media, groundbreaking apps, and digital marketing? Or are they heavily involved in the use of artificial intelligence to generate significant cost-savings? In other words: In what ways are you looking for this tech-savvy director to add value to the board?

➢ **Ownership considerations, where applicable** –Where a majority shareholder, dual-class share structure and/or a third party (such as an investor or government body) has the right to appoint one or more of the company's directors, this also needs to be factored into board composition. Sometimes, this expands the size of the board: Many boards of family-controlled companies, for example, are somewhat larger in order to facilitate having several family directors at the board table, while nonetheless ensuring that the board's composition includes all of the other expertise considered important to govern the company effectively.

Pitfalls to Avoid

In working through a Board 2.0 exercise, two assumptions about board composition design sometimes arise, which need to be debunked:

i. **A board is not a shadow management team**: Some respondents want to fill in the circles of their Board 2.0 template so that every board seat matches up with one of the CEO's direct reports in terms of expertise – a finance person, a lawyer, a marketing expert, a human resources specialist, etc. But this reflects a misunderstanding of the board's oversight role. The board is required to oversee the company, not each senior executive individually; that's the CEO's job. Typically, breadth is more important (even in areas of functional expertise like finance) than narrow subject matter expertise because of the range of issues most boards have to confront. Moreover, there may be expertise appropriate at the board table that wouldn't typically reside on an executive team (e.g., an economist, a strategy consultant).

ii. **A board is not a focus group**: Some people populate their Board 2.0 template based on consumer segments. But this is the criteria for a focus group, not a Board of Directors. Of course, it's a great idea for a children's apparel company to have some parents on the board. But those parents also need to be seasoned business executives, well able to challenge the integration plans for an M&A transaction, identify risks of a capital financing proposal and/or determine the key performance metrics that should be included in the CEO's compensation plan – along with offering their insights on some of the company's marketing issues from a parent's perspective. It's great to combine functional expertise with consumer demographics as this can add tremendous value; however, recruiting board members on the basis of customer segmentation alone is far too shallow.

Board Experience

Board experience should be a consideration in optimal board composition design. However, this is not a straightforward issue; not every director needs to have board experience. Many younger directors and those actively employed in executive roles (a sitting CEO, COO, or CFO) will never have served on another board – but often make excellent directors. They should certainly not be excluded for this reason. After all, every great new director needs their first board seat!

In designing the optimal board, some proportion of the directors should have experience serving on other boards – and for very practical reasons: The "line between governance and management" is something new directors often struggle with when they have not served on a board previously. On those rare occasions when I've worked with boards whose directors had very little board experience, they often spent an inordinate amount of time on micro-management issues instead of focusing at a proper oversight level.

Board experience also comes into play relative to board leadership. Occasionally, a very strong candidate is able to effectively assume a board leadership role with no prior board experience. But most directors include "board experience" as one of their criteria for a Non-Executive Board Chair or Lead Director, and for obvious reasons: A firm grasp of board process – gained from serving on other boards – can be particularly useful in fulfilling many board leadership responsibilities, including setting board agendas, conducting the annual CEO evaluation, leading CEO succession planning, etc.

Diversity

Diversity is an extremely important consideration in board composition. Gender diversity became a paramount consideration for many boards over the past decade, with initiatives such as the 30% Club and others gaining traction in expanding the number of board seats held by women. Racial diversity has perhaps never been a more important focal point than it is today. Undoubtedly, many US Nominating Committees are currently considering whether and how best to increase the proportion of African Americans and other directors of color serving on their boards.

Allocating a "diversity seat" in composing a Board 2.0 may seem like the obvious answer. However, this approach implies that not a single seat in the optimally designed Board 2.0 (which focuses on expertise and backgrounds) could be filled by a diversity candidate. Not only is this largely untrue in the twenty-first century, it is an approach that smacks of tokenism and even marginalization, as if to say: "Here's our core board in terms of optimal expertise – plus a diversity director." Directors who serve to diversify the board's composition need to be every bit as core to the board's makeup as all the other directors at the board table – only in this way will the board truly function as an effective governance team.

In practical terms, there may not be a rich pool of diversity candidates to meet the requirements of *every* seat defined from a Board 2.0 exercise. Some board seats may be tough to find candidates for at all – and talent pools are always deeper for diverse board candidates in some areas of expertise than they are for others. This is a consideration that needs to be taken into account in populating the board while achieving both diversity goals and optimal composition from the standpoint of backgrounds and expertise. For example, a director search focused on finance or technology backgrounds will nearly always surface well-qualified diverse candidates. In some industries, such as retail, diversity candidates with operational experience are plentiful; in other industries, such as mining, the talent pool for diversity candidates may be quite shallow. That said, for *any* board comprised of seven or more directors, it's tough to imagine a scenario where strong diversity candidates could not be found for at least three or four of the board seats developed through a Board 2.0 exercise – if not many more.

Any board looking to expand its proportion of diverse directors can navigate this issue by balancing talent pools against recruitment priorities. Let's say the board's top director recruitment priority is a former CEO from the industry – but that's a small pool of candidates to begin with, and none of them are diverse. What then, are the secondary and tertiary recruitment priorities? Do these yield richer talent pools for diversity candidates? Or perhaps one of the current directors haven't been pulling their weight – and has a finance background that the board would want to replace if they either stepped down or were not re-nominated. Finance is often a deep talent pool for diversity. Recruiting in this direction could be a smart pre-emptive strategy, as the underperforming director's days may be numbered, and a very capable diversity candidate may join the board as a result.

Defining the expertise that would add real value at the board table and *then* seeking out diverse candidates who meet these criteria has proven to be an effective strategy for many boards. Let me offer two examples, both of which involve S&P1500 boards who had prioritized recruitment of an African American director:

Case Study #1: The board of an athletic retailer had clear priorities for their next board recruit: They wanted someone with deep technology expertise, specifically a very senior role in digital marketing at a large organization. They wanted a younger director; most of their board was over 55. They wanted an African American; they had two Hispanic board members and several female directors, but this was a gap in their composition. And a big "nice to have" was that this person should be somewhat athletic – a runner, a cyclist, someone who plays pick-up basketball or coaches baseball as a hobby, or who was a competitive athlete in their youth.

When the Nominating Committee Chair gave the board's search consultant a "head's up" that they'd be starting this search once the full board had discussed the board evaluation, she replied, "You guys are looking for a unicorn!" But the board stuck to their guns through the evaluation discussion. As one director said, "Look, we've defined the person we really want – and we all agree. So let's shoot for someone like this! If we can't find anyone, okay then, we'll make some compromises. But let's at least give it a shot and see what happens."

After the meeting, directors and executives gathered in the hotel bar and started brainstorming. As wine and beer flowed, so did the suggestions – and the Chair of the Nominating Committee walked out with four recommendations that "seem pretty close to what we're after." Moreover, these names surfaced because someone on the board or in the company's executive team knew each of these four candidates – and offered to contact them and explore their interest in being considered.

In the end, this board was faced with a tough decision: Two of the candidates were outstanding – and some directors wanted to recruit them both. The Nominating Committee had to make a choice. They offered the board seat to an African American executive in his 40s who had been a college athlete in his youth. He ran a major division of a large Silicon Valley technology company. Not only did this new director prove to be an outstanding board member, in a few years' time, he became the Lead Director.

Case Study #2: An NYSE-listed financial services company had recruited an African American director in the late 1990s when he retired from a Wall Street firm. Eventually, he hit the board's mandatory retirement age. The Nominating Committee sought to replace him – but the ex-Wall Streeter that rose to the top of the candidate list this round was a white woman, who impressed board members with her expertise on capital structure issues and engaging personality.

Having another female director was considered an asset. But the board remained sensitive to the fact they now lacked a director of color. Consequently, they asked their search firm for a list of African American board candidates, with little else to go on in terms of background or expertise. The headhunter dutifully produced a lengthy list of highly accomplished African American lawyers, ex-politicians, academics, and executives from various industries. Interviews commenced – but none of these candidates seemed to get any traction.

Around this time, the board undertook a board evaluation that incorporated a Board 2.0 exercise. This enabled the board to reach consensus on skills and expertise they needed to prioritize in director recruitment: A SOX financial expert who could back up and eventually replace the Audit Committee Chair when he retired, preferably a current or retired Chief Financial Officer – and optimally, someone with a banking background.

They returned to the search firm and asked for a list of candidates who met these criteria – specifying that they wanted to see several African American candidates included. When the new candidate list was compiled, the Chairman circulated it to all board members and corporate executives, asking if they knew anyone on the list. One of the corporate SVPs immediately called the Chairman. He was excited by one of the names – a female African American Chief Financial Officer with a banking background who he'd worked with in the past. He offered a ringing endorsement: "Donna is one of the most intelligent, insightful, and genuinely nice people I've ever had the pleasuring of working with. If we could bring her on to our board, I think she'd be outstanding!"

The SVP's endorsement caused the Chairman to place Donna at the top of the interview list. After they met her, directors quickly reached consensus: "Donna was night and day compared to the lawyers and professors we'd been talking to before! She really knows our business – she understands the market issues, she knew our competitors, she talked a lot about the implications of some of the proposed regulatory changes. You could tell right away that Donna would be an amazing director who'd add a lot of value to our board."

"Our problem," the Chair reflected, "was that we initially went about our recruitment process the wrong way: We knew we wanted to see African American director candidates, but we never specified what we were after in terms of background or expertise. Consequently, our headhunter gave us a range of accomplished people – but none of them seemed like a good fit. Once we defined the type of experience we needed and **_then_** asked the headhunter to include African American candidates who met these criteria, we found a great candidate very quickly."

Several boards I've worked with recently have found some very impressive board candidates – particularly diversity candidates – by supplementing the efforts of their search firm with recommendations from their business network. Typically, this begins by tapping into board members and company executives (as in Case Study #1) and expands to the board's advisors – external auditors, legal counsel, compensation consultants, and others. One Nominating Committee Chair explained his process: "I went to our law firm, our strategy consulting firm, and our compensation consultants. I told them we wanted a Hispanic director with a background in branding/marketing, preferably someone with global experience. Some offered suggestions right away; others asked their colleagues and came back to me a few days later with recommendations surfaced from that process. Within a week, I had five more candidate names to add to our headhunter's list – and some of these people had incredible backgrounds. What's more, our advisors had worked with several of these people and recommended them from personal experience, which carried a lot of weight from my perspective."

Personal Qualities/Characteristics

Just because a director has a great background and highly desirable expertise doesn't mean they will be effective as a board member. No matter how stellar their experience, any director who routinely shows up unprepared, constantly delves into minutiae and adopts an antagonistic tone in debates with board colleagues and management is not the kind of person any company wants or needs at its board table.

Notwithstanding their importance, personal qualities/characteristics are omitted from a Board 2.0 exercise. This is because these are qualities that **all** board members should have. No one would allocate one board seat for a director with "sound judgment" and another for a director who is a "good team player"; these traits should be expected of each and every member of the board.

> **Case Study #3:** Some years back, I worked with the board of a conglomerate in Asia whose director criteria were almost entirely comprised of personal qualities/characteristics. They had some very fine people on their board, all of whom were extremely accomplished. However, only a handful of directors had the expertise necessary to challenge management in a meaningful way – and many felt that the CEO had been "running roughshod" over the board for years. Despite their impressive backgrounds, only a few directors – one of whom had run a massive division of a large global company, himself – could effectively counter the CEO's responses to board concerns and expose problems. One of the outcomes of their board evaluation involved changing their approach on director recruitment criteria – and actively seeking out new board members with operational backgrounds at major global companies.

It is much easier to approach director recruitment in four stages:

i.   define the optimal background/expertise the board is looking for;

ii. ensure the search includes candidates that would meet the board's diversity objectives, wherever feasible;

iii. ensure there are enough directors with board experience and if not, factor this into the search; and

iv. screen for personal qualities/characteristics during the interviews and with references.

Nominating Committee members involved in director interviews need to ask thoughtful questions designed to get some insights about the candidate's personal qualities. References are also essential. While interviews provide only a snapshot, they can often be telling. Here are two examples provided by Board Chairs of NYSE-listed companies, both of whom "screened out" some otherwise promising candidates on the basis of "red flags" that emerged during their interviews:

> **Case Study #4:** "I arrived at the candidate's office with the Chair of the Governance Committee. On paper, this guy looked great! The interview was an hour in length. He spoke for about 57 of those 60 minutes. He simply would not shut up! Whenever I or my colleague tried to get a word in edgewise, to ask him a few questions, he'd say, "Just let me finish my thought." Then he'd carry on. At no point did he stop and say, "Okay, I've finished now. Did you have a question?" When the hour was finally up, he escorted us to the elevator. During the descent, the other director turned to me and said, 'Could you imagine that guy in one of our board meetings? Nobody else would have a chance to say anything!' That was the end of his candidacy.

> **Case Study #5:** For nearly two years out company had been dealing with an activist fund that advocated the sale of one of our divisions. Because our industry was cyclical, the board felt strongly that this division helped to offset the inevitable "down cycles" of our main business. Numerous stories about our squabble with XXX Capital had appeared in the *Wall Street Journal*; if you googled our company name, a long list of articles about this issue quickly emerged.

> I was interviewing a director candidate who had some great credentials. However, she was not from our industry and had never served on a board before. I wasn't fussed about that; it just meant she'd have to put in a fair bit of effort to learn our business. I had to do that several years ago, myself, when I joined the board of a company outside my industry. I knew what was necessary and was confident that someone with her credentials would step up.

During the interview, I asked the candidate for her thoughts on the shareholder activism issue with XXX Capital. She gave me a blank look. "XXX Capital? What's that all about?" "The sale of our electronics business," I replied. She shook her head, "I don't know anything about that, so I wouldn't want to comment."

She obviously hadn't done any homework whatsoever to prepare for the interview – or to learn anything about what was going on with our company. The most preliminary Google search would have unearthed a myriad of articles around this topic. Consequently, I was skeptical about whether she'd invest the time and effort required to learn about our industry if we offered her a board seat. Although she was initially our top candidate, we ultimately chose someone else who not only had solid credentials but had clearly put in some effort to prepare. This candidate offered some very well-considered opinions around the XXX Capital debate in her interview and on a range of other issues impacting our company.

Personal qualities/characteristics are clearly important considerations in director selection. But ongoing director performance management is critical too. And this is something most boards do poorly, if they attempt to do it at all. PwC's research, mentioned earlier, suggests that this is an issue that boards need to pay more attention to: 49% of the 693 board members PwC surveyed believe at least one of their fellow directors needs to be replaced – and 21% think that two or more need to go.[14] These results suggest that half of all US boards are currently wrestling with a problem that entails either:

i.   **An expertise issue** – the director simply doesn't have the kind of relevant background to make worthwhile contributions. This problem can be readily tackled with Board 2.0;

ii. **A performance issue** – the director has a great background but some kind of behavioral problem is getting in the way. Because directors are typically successful businesspeople with a myriad of impressive achievements, addressing individual performance issues can be awkward. Using director evaluations to tackle these sorts of issues will be discussed in-depth in Chapter Four. Chapter Four will also introduce a concept that many boards may find useful to incorporate into their Director Orientation Program: The New Director 360, which can nip performance problems in the bud, before they become significant concerns;

iii. **Both expertise and performance issues** – the director's background doesn't allow them to make a lot of meaningful contributions *and* the problem is exacerbated by shortcomings in behavior/performance.

What Happens if an Incumbent Director's Expertise is Excluded from Board 2.0?

This outcome is almost inevitable, because Board 2.0 is focused on the future: Of course, there will be some different skill sets considered more important in Board 2.0 than those that are resident at the board table today. Companies grow and morph over time; what may have been the perfect board background seven or eight years ago is now overshadowed by other business priorities.

Some momentary drama can emerge when one or more of the current directors' backgrounds don't show up in Board 2.0. However, there are two things to bear in mind when this occurs: First, Board 2.0 is the optimal board designed to govern the company in three years' time – not next week. Second, this outcome has an upside – particularly given the propensity of many boards to ignore director performance issues.

How quickly a director who doesn't fit Board 2.0 departs from the board can depend on a number of factors. The Nominating Committee can either accelerate or defer board turnover, as they deem appropriate, with Board 2.0 creating a useful lever the Committee can use in this process. In practical terms, it is nearly always the director's performance and contributions as a board member that determines this timing:

14 PwC, "Turning crisis into opportunity", 14.

❖ A director who hasn't been carrying their weight, whose contributions are fairly marginal, and whose skill set is nowhere to be seen in Board 2.0 will generally be leaving the board sooner rather than later. Most Nominating Committees begin their work towards creating Board 2.0 with some director recruitment efforts; no one is asked to leave immediately, and the board size temporarily expands. But it's made clear that the expansion *is* temporary, a first step in the Board 2.0 transition. In these circumstances, don't be at all surprised if a year down the road, the underperforming director – who also isn't a fit for Board 2.0 – offers to resign. After all, the writing is on the wall and most directors in these circumstances prefer to step down graciously instead of being asked to leave. If they don't voluntarily resign, Board 2.0 nonetheless provides the Nominating Committee with a leverage point to reference when they explain to the director why they are not being re-nominated: "As you know, we need to make this change sooner or later, and now that we have recruited two new directors …"

❖ On the other hand, a high-performing director who makes extremely valuable board contributions will likely continue to be re-nominated for some time to come, regardless of the fact that this director's expertise isn't included in Board 2.0's design. Director re-nomination, after all, is entirely at the discretion of the Nominating Committee. Does anyone care if the board size expands by one seat during the Board 2.0 transition so as to ensure that one of the board's most outstanding directors is still at the table? In such circumstances, the Board Chair or Governance Committee Chair should sit down with the high-performing director immediately after the board's discussion of Board 2.0 to avoid a peremptory resignation of a board member nobody wants to lose. Make it clear that in the board's view, this director adds tremendous value; even though they may not fit Board 2.0, there is no desire for this person to leave.

Board 2.0 vs. Board Skills Matrix

As many directors are familiar with the use of a Board Skills Matrix, I'm often asked about the differences between a Skills Matrix and Board 2.0:

➢ **Board 2.0 is Forward-Looking.** The Board Skills Matrix is far more of an investor relations tool than a board succession planning tool, in that it focuses largely on current board composition. Many companies include their Skills Matrix in their proxy circular and list their current directors' names beside it – ticking off each category in the matrix where the director's background is a "fit". Board 2.0, on the other hand, focuses on the optimal board to govern the company in 3–5 years' time. These are two different questions – and consequently, they produce different results. This is the reason why some boards use both.

➢ **Board 2.0 is Specific.** A Board Skills Matrix typically uses general categories (such as Finance or Technology). Personal characteristics are also sometimes included in a Board Skills Matrix, along with other general capabilities most boards would expect nearly all their directors to have, such as "Leadership" and "Strategy". Board 2.0, on the other hand, is far more specific – and draws out the reasons why a particular background is considered important.

➢ **Board 2.0 Forces Prioritization.** There are a finite number of seats around the board table of Board 2.0, which forces decisions about what's really important: How is each board seat most wisely "spent" so as to optimize the overall composition of the future board? A Board Skills Matrix, on the other hand, is typically comprised of a long list of categories with no evident limit.

Board Composition Benchmarking

Another tool that can be very useful in board composition design is Board Composition Benchmarking. This can be either added to a Board 2.0 exercise or conducted as a stand-alone project.

The concept is simple: take the peer group developed for executive compensation purposes and conduct an analysis of the composition of each peer company's board. A sample of the output from a board benchmarking exercise is found at Appendix C. Board benchmarking studies provide insights not only into directors' backgrounds/expertise, but also into diversity, age, tenure, board experience, and other composition issues. A review of peer board governance policies (such as director retirement policies, mandatory resignation on job change, etc.) can also be incorporated into this analysis.

The point of this benchmarking exercise isn't to suggest that your board's composition should mirror that of other companies in your industry. In fact, you may find the results eye-opening in terms of some of the backgrounds of people sitting on your competitors' boards. Benchmarking simply provides another data point for the board to consider in developing Board 2.0 – and nearly every board I've used it with found this exercise to be worthwhile and enlightening.

In Summary............

Initially developed for boards undergoing major transitions (mergers, IPOs, significant changes in business/strategy), a Board 2.0 exercise can readily be incorporated into an interview-based board evaluation, whereby all directors and corporate executives design the ultimate board to govern the company in 3–5 years' time. Every board's optimal make-up will and should differ, reflecting the company's business model, stage of growth, ownership structure, and corporate strategy. Diversity, personal qualities/ characteristics and other factors that are equally important in optimizing board composition can then be incorporated into director selection. The pace of transition to achieve Board 2.0 is entirely within the discretion of the Nominating Committee – and may be accelerated or deferred as the Committee deems appropriate. Board composition benchmarking is a data-driven analytical tool that can be used to supplement a Board 2.0 exercise.

Chapter Four

Director Evaluations that are Genuinely Worthwhile

Director Performance Management:
The Biggest Gap in Governance Today

I'VE MENTIONED THE PwC study several times already in this book because it's important. In 2012, the same study was considered groundbreaking in US corporate governance because 31% of directors at that time felt at least one of their fellow board members should be replaced.[15] The trend has been continuing upwards over the past decade, such that 49% of 693 respondents in the 2020 PwC survey now feel that way – and 21% think that two or more need to go.[16] The climb in "problem directors" evidenced by the PwC results underscores a simple fact: Most boards don't do a very good job when it comes to director performance management.

The term "director development" has become synonymous with director education: Sending board members to governance courses and having them participate in webinars on a range of current topics. There's nothing wrong with that. Keeping directors on top of the latest trends and developments in governance is an important component of board-building. But it's one-dimensional – and, by itself –wholly inadequate if the larger objective is to build a high-performing governance team. Anyone who's serious about getting to the top of their game professionally in any endeavor needs constructive feedback that serves to confirm what they're doing well and identifies areas for continuous improvement.

Many boards only consider director evaluations when they have a "problem director". That's not necessarily a bad thing; it's far better than continuing to ignore the situation. As the PwC research underscores, more boards need to step up to performance issues – and this can be one way to do it. But director evaluations can and should be much more than a trap for underperforming board members. What about the rest of the directors? Are they largely to be bystanders in an all-out effort to "get rid of Director X"? A really worthwhile director evaluation should provide *all* board members with meaningful and genuinely insightful feedback. Reinforcing the strengths and contributions of your boardroom stars can be every bit as important in board-building as censuring the under-performers.

These two examples provide very different but equally useful illustrations of this point:

---

15 PwC, "Insights from the Boardroom 2012", *PwC's Annual Corporate Directors Survey* (October, 2012), 8. Accessed October 20, 2020, https://www.pwc.com/us/en/corporate-governance/annual-corporate-directors-survey/assets/pdf/pwc-annual-corporate-directors-survey.pdf.

16 PwC, "Turning crisis into opportunity", 14.

Case Study #1: A young tech-savvy director had joined the board of a financial services company just over a year ago. This was his first board. When he was being recruited, directors advised him to "shake things up" a bit. But he sensed he'd already gone a bit too far. About six months in, he'd challenged the CEO on the use of contract employees, a burgeoning practice. The CEO seemed taken aback – and not at all receptive to his concerns – first dodging and then dismissing his question. At the next meeting, a technology issue emerged – and this time, the new director was determined not to "pull in his horns" if the CEO got defensive. But the result was a heated boardroom exchange that clearly made everyone uncomfortable. The new board member had said very little in the board meetings since that time.

In his director evaluation, board members acknowledged that the new director had taken a fairly aggressive, even sarcastic, tone with the CEO – and admonished him for that. But they were also quick to underscore that both of his contentious points had been extremely good ones. They commended him for his insights and were very clear in their advice: "Okay, things went a little off the rails at the June meeting. But now, he seems to have pulled back entirely. And that's no good at all! We want to hear from him! He has terrific insights! A little more diplomacy might not hurt in making his points – but he has the makings of a really great director, and the last thing we want is for him to take a back seat in our board meetings."

Case Study #2: A global company based in Asia was emerging from a financial scandal, which had forced the replacement of the entire board three years earlier. The new Audit Committee Chair – a former Big Four partner – had worked tirelessly on the financial restatements. In her own interview, she explained that there were times when she barely saw her family for weeks on end and had spent her last two vacations on lengthy calls with the external auditors. When she received the glowing feedback provided by her board colleagues – citing specific examples of important decisions she'd made and steps she'd taken to navigate the crisis – she was moved almost to tears. "Can I share this with my daughters?" she asked, "I am one of the only female Audit Committee Chairs of a major company in this country. Knowing that I have earned this kind of respect from the other board members for my efforts means the world to me."

Now, one might argue that it's the role of the Board Chair to address these situations: To ensure that the Audit Committee Chair in Case Study #2 knew how much her efforts were appreciated and to intercede with the new director, who clearly needed some coaching, in Case Study #1. And you would not be wrong! Director performance management *is* the responsibility of the Board Chair – and it's one of the toughest facets of the Chair's role.

Some Board Chairs do a great job in this regard and build their boards into superlative governance teams. Others, however, both ignore performance problems and seldom acknowledge great contributions. In the 2020 PwC survey, performance management was the area where directors gave board leadership their lowest scores, with one in four (25%) of respondents indicating that leadership is either "not very or not at all effective" in this regard.[17]

Even if the Board Chair is doing an outstanding job in this respect, there's nothing wrong with supplementing the Chair's efforts with a structured process to solicit constructive feedback from all board members every three years or so – a process called a director evaluation. In fact, most Board Chairs who are true champions heartily endorse this practice because they understand that it provides a broader range of feedback for their directors that can advance their own efforts in board-building.

---

17 PwC, "Turning Crisis into Opportunity", 15.

What About those "Problem Directors"?

Will a director evaluation process solve the problem of an underperforming director? Well, that depends. Not the answer you probably wanted, but please bear with me, as there are a number of factors that come into play around this issue and it's by no means a straightforward one.

Most directors take their peers' feedback very seriously when it's presented in a constructive, actionable way. This is exactly what all board members should receive from an effective director evaluation process, as illustrated in the sample Director Feedback Reports in Appendix D-1 and D-2. If the problem is a behavioral issue – the "problem director" shows up at meetings unprepared, "hogs air-time" in board meetings by weighing in on every issue or takes an abrasive tone in challenging management and fellow directors – they will very likely try make some changes for the better.

But let's be brutally honest: In many "problem director" scenarios, the real objective is ***not*** to change behavior. It's to get Director X to leave the board – in as graceful a way as possible and preferably with little fuss. Does that happen? Yes, it does. But not every time – and in many cases not without some further interventions by the Board Chair and/or the Nominating Committee. I'll offer several illustrations of the different scenarios that typically play out in this regard.

To start these examples at one extreme, I have had two situations (both, interestingly, in the Southern US) where three directors resigned simply because the board "threatened" to introduce a director evaluation process. These board members obviously had a pretty good idea that they weren't going to like the outcome, so they chose to leave the board rather than go through the evaluation process. Needless to say, no one tried to stop them. In fact, these were the very people that board leadership had rather hoped would exit the board as an outcome of this process, so they were delighted. But this is very rare and hasn't happened in many years.

I've had several occasions where directors have told me during their evaluation interview that they've decided to resign from the board. This most often happens where the director evaluation is paired with something like a Board 2.0 exercise: In preparing for the interview, the director reflects on their "fit" with the optimal board composition, realizes that they are perhaps not the strongest member of the board, considers whether they are really enjoying being on the board – and decides to do "the honorable thing" by offering to step down right away, even before receiving any feedback. Again, there was seldom much opposition when this occurred and more often a sense of relief that the director had the professionalism and self-awareness to be proactive in this regard.

There have also been many instances – and even more of these – where a director resigned shortly after receiving their feedback. This typically occurred where problems that surfaced in the director's individual evaluation involved conflicts of interest or where the director's feedback confirmed what they were already thinking. These two cases illustrate the latter point:

Case Study #3: This involved a well-respected sitting CEO who was serving on an outside board. He was having trouble balancing the demands of both roles. Directors provided feedback that acknowledged the tremendous value of his perspectives – but also expressed concern that he'd seemed "pre-occupied" and "distracted" for quite some time and was no longer making the valuable contributions he was capable of. His own company was in trouble, and he knew he hadn't been carrying his weight in the boardroom. This feedback from his peers was a graceful way out – and he wholeheartedly agreed with their comments. He spoke to the Lead Director and resigned from the board with no hard feelings. In fact, he respected his fellow directors even more for calling the question. And they respected him for doing the right thing by stepping down when he honestly recognized that he couldn't devote more time and energy to board affairs.

Case Study #4: A director whose expertise was primarily in commercial real estate had been appointed to the board of an agribusiness by a pension fund with which he'd had a long relationship. Agribusiness held little appeal for him, but he felt he had to say "yes" when the fund offered him this board seat three years earlier. When his feedback focused almost entirely on steps he should consider to learn more about the industry, he was honest: he had no interest in making these efforts. Instead, he spoke to the head of the fund, who switched him to another board assignment.

In most cases, however, Director X receives their feedback and life goes on. Most of the time, Director X will take steps to try to address any of the problems raised. And while this nearly always yields some improvement, in other cases, the results are only marginal. Other times, there is honestly very little that Director X can do: Perhaps it is an issue of currency, where Director X has been retired for many years during which business practices have changed tremendously. Or perhaps Director X simply doesn't have the background/expertise that the board really needs at this juncture. Other times, Director X just can't stop berating management over some "pet issue", even though feedback made it abundantly clear that people were tired of this. In all these situations, the director evaluation came into play at the time of a decision around Director X's re-nomination. Where Director X left the board, it was typically due to one of the following three scenarios:

- Frequently, Director X took the initiative and informed board leadership that they had decided not to stand for another term. After all, if the 'writing is on the wall' many directors prefer to step down graciously, and the director evaluation has put Director X on notice.

- Sometimes the Board Chair convinced Director X to resign – referencing the director evaluation. The Chair might have suggested that Director X would do better to resign before the question came before the Committee, as the outcome seems inevitable.

- On other occasions, the Nominating Committee had to make a tough decision: Director X neither tendered a resignation nor took up the Board Chair's suggestion. The Committee then had to squarely face the re-nomination question. When this happened, Committee members often pointed out that when the director evaluation put Director X "on notice" about the problems, they either refused or were unable to address them in a meaningful way and now the Committee honestly felt Director X should be replaced.

The latter two are seldom pleasant situations – nor are they as graceful as a spontaneous "gestalt moment" whereby Director X realizes they should leave the board. In many cases, however, the director evaluation serves as the lay-up, but board leadership or the Nominating Committee is nonetheless required to follow through. Let's face it: Some Board Chairs don't have the stomach to sit down with a problem director and try to convince them to resign from the board. And some Nominating Committees don't have the appetite to make that tough call: "I just can't bring myself to vote her out; in only two more years she'll hit our board retirement age." In the 2020 PwC survey, 20% of respondents indicated that board leadership was unwilling to have difficult conversations with underperforming directors.[18] Moreover, only 12% said their board had chosen not to re-nominate a director and only 14% indicated that their board "provided counsel to a director"[19]

---

18 Ibid, 14.

19 Ibid, 15

In short, using a director evaluation process to deal with a "problem director", who most feel should leave the board, can and does work. However, resolving the situation sometimes comes down to the board's intestinal fortitude to have a tough conversation and make a difficult decision once the director evaluation has laid the groundwork for this to occur.

Director Evaluations and "Tone at the Top"

Director evaluations are a far more important tool in board-building than merely serving as a lever to eject a problem director from the boardroom. They can and should be an integral part of building your governance team. Effective director evaluation feedback can polish off rough edges, reinforce important contributions, and help your good directors to become even better. It can underscore the strengths of your boardroom stars, making them shine even brighter. But perhaps most important of all: when they're credible and well-designed, director evaluations set the right "tone at the top."

Any board that insists on robust CEO and senior executive evaluations – and holds management's feet to the fire on performance, as they should – needs to think seriously about ensuring it has adopted both a robust board evaluation and a director evaluation that's genuinely worthwhile. These processes underscore the board's commitment to accountability and performance. Executives sincerely respect boards that step up in this regard and typically disparage (however quietly) those that don't or who introduce such watered-down versions that they ultimately impugn the board's credibility and that of board leadership.

Designing an Effective Director Evaluation

Whether your objectives involve implementing a governance practice that can be genuinely worthwhile for all your board members, tackling a director performance issue that's weighing down the entire board, setting the right tone at the top, or some combination of all three, it's essential to adopt an effective director evaluation process. Otherwise, none of those objectives are likely to be achieved.

More than 20 years ago, when I had the privilege of undertaking my first director evaluation, we used a survey form with 1–5 ratings and write-in comments. In fact, this was the process I used for director evaluations over the next five years, with some short follow-up phone calls added into the mix. At the time, it was considered "leading edge".

With the survey approach, directors would read over their individual reports and comment, "Okay, I'm a 3.2. What is that supposed to tell me?" Write-in comments were often vague, sometimes rambling, and occasionally downright nasty. Follow-up phone calls clarified the written comments and frequently drew out some genuinely worthwhile feedback. But I'd typically hang up wondering why we hadn't just interviewed all the board members in the first place. Only when we engaged in conversations did we elicit the sort of genuinely valuable feedback that would have directors nodding and saying, "This is actually a very good point!" or "Wow! I never realized that was how I was coming across. I need to change that!"

Consequently, I started to change my process for director evaluations about 15 years ago – and have continued to experiment ever since. The New Director 360, discussed later in this chapter, is my latest innovation. Based on my experience to date, these are some of the key considerations in designing a genuinely effective director evaluation process:

➢ **An Interview format lends itself particularly well to director evaluations.** This enables the interviewer to probe until they elicit the type of constructive, actionable feedback that is genuinely worthwhile for recipients. For director feedback to be truly effective:

- **It should be specific and constructive** – enabling the recipient to readily understand both the strengths/contributions that are being extolled and potential areas for improvement. Sample Director Feedback Reports, found in Appendices D-1 and D-2, are illustrative of this point.

- **It should be balanced** – the hallmark of an effective director evaluation is that *all* directors receive both positive feedback to reinforce their strengths *and* advice on where they could be even more effective. Perhaps ironically, it is often the best board members who most value suggestions for improvement; while "problem directors" are far more likely to accept negative feedback when they also receive some genuine appreciation for what they've done well.

➤ **Protocols should be sent out in advance.** This gets directors thinking about what they'll say relative to each of their colleagues – and ultimately yields richer and more thoughtful feedback, replete with useful examples. I prefer general questions, followed by probing, about each director's major strengths and contributions; then advice on what might make this director even more effective than they are today. I've tried rolling through a litany of questions such as, "Does he/she seem well-prepared for meetings?" "Does he/she ask good questions?" "Is he/she respectful in challenging other board members or management in the meetings?" However, I always found that these types of functional questions ate up a lot of interview time before we got to the crux of the really important issues.

➤ **Use of an external facilitator.** This ensures confidentiality and typically fosters greater candor, which is essential to an effective director evaluation process; interviewees are nearly always more open with an external facilitator. Concerns about confidentiality noted in Chapter Two relative to board evaluations are amplified when it comes to director evaluations, given the more personal and therefore more sensitive nature of the feedback. Using a third party also prevents some directors from dismissing negative feedback by attributing it to a personal bias of the Board Chair or any other internal interviewer.

Having director evaluations externally facilitated every few years by no means detracts from the Chair's responsibility to regularly discuss director performance issues with board members. On the contrary, it typically serves to reinforce some of the Chair's feedback, demonstrating that a concern or accolade previously mentioned by the Chair is not just a personal perspective but a widely held view.

➤ **The CEO should be included.** The process described in this chapter is sometimes referred to as a "director peer review" – because directors provide commentary about their peers on the board and receive feedback from them.

As the CEO is typically a board member, they should always be included in the director evaluation process. However, it must be underscored that this process is not a CEO evaluation, which is a much different exercise that focuses on the role of the CEO in running the company and typically includes KPI metrics and many other components. During a director evaluation, I tend to focus feedback for the CEO around their effectiveness in working with the board. This can yield extremely useful insights for any CEO – particularly a new CEO who has been in the role two years or less – as it serves to reinforce positive aspects of the CEO/board relationship and/or provide an early warning signal, if there are problems. If the CEO also serves as Chair, obviously the questions are then targeted towards their role in facilitating board meetings, designing effective board agendas and otherwise fulfilling the requirements of board leadership.

Senior executives do not typically participate in individual director evaluations, even though many boards now include them in board evaluations. However, this may change over time. The New Director 360, which will be introduced later in this chapter, broadens the range of respondents to include both top executives and advisors to the board or board committees, such as compensation consultants and external auditors.

➢ **Determine how far the director evaluation feedback will be shared.** This is a crucial issue – and one that needs to be considered at the outset of any director evaluation process. Typically, the draft Director Evaluation Reports are shared and discussed with the Board Chair and Governance Committee Chair before they are finalized. This achieves two things: (i) two key board leaders understand the feedback for each director; and (ii) it allows them to raise any concerns before the reports are finalized. For example, if some of the feedback seems unclear or if there is a sample quote that can easily be attributed to one of the board members, this can be addressed. During this review process, the Chair's draft feedback report is typically shared with the Governance Committee Chair and vice versa.

Some boards – particularly those embarking on an individual director evaluation process for the first time – limit the feedback exclusively to the director for whom the report is prepared. Neither the report nor any of the feedback from it may be disclosed to anyone else – including the Board Chair or Governance Committee Chair. This means that the director evaluation process will be used *solely* for the professional development of their board members and plays no part in re-nomination decisions. While somewhat unconventional, this practice serves to alleviate some of the initial angst many boards have around director evaluations when they're introducing or upgrading this process. Even though no one else was privy to it, directors typically took their peers' feedback seriously and acted on it in these scenarios. It should be noted that in most of these cases, however, the board did not have any real "problem directors"; they largely wanted to amplify the merits of the governance team they had.

By contrast, other boards that have chosen to factor the director evaluation into their re-nomination decisions sometimes insist that the full Nominating Committee be given access to either the individual director feedback reports or a summary of them. This, by the way, is not indicative of the fact that a board anticipates having to make a tough decision about an underperforming director; in nearly every case in which this feedback was shared more broadly, that was not a factor at all. Provided that Committee members are respectful of the confidentiality of the feedback, which is generally the case, this process can also work well.

However, the practice of sharing individual director evaluation reports with the full board and discussing them openly in a board meeting has some significant downsides. This may be a "more transparent" approach, but it can create awkwardness and even embarrassment for some board members. It probably won't accomplish much in terms of board team building either.

All that said, it is entirely at each board's discretion how far the director feedback will be shared – and whether it will factor into re-nomination decisions or not. However, it is important to make a decision about these questions early on – and well before the interviews get started, as interviewees inevitably ask this question.

➢ **Debrief meetings to review the Director Evaluation Reports with recipients are essential.** Rather than simply sending each director their feedback report, it's far more productive to sit down and walk through the report with each recipient. This allows for questions, clarification, and challenges – all of which are important for the process to be genuinely worthwhile. Personal meetings are always good and can be easily scheduled around a board meeting, as they are typically quite short. But in the age of Zoom, it's possible to do this by videoconference using the screen share feature, which is even easier.

Occasionally, I've worked with Board Chairs who wanted to personally deliver the feedback reports to their directors. These Chairs understood the importance of having a third party gather the feedback, conduct the analysis, and prepare the individual reports. But, as the leader of the board and the "coach of the governance team", they wanted to sit down with each director for their feedback conversations. While relatively rare, this practice typically worked out well, particularly if directors were given an opportunity to follow up with the external facilitator subsequent to the meeting with the Chair. This allowed them to clarify key points and ask more nuanced questions about the feedback they received. In these situations, the Chair's own feedback is typically delivered by the facilitator.

> **Discoverability issues (addressed in Chapter Two) also apply to director evaluations**. Director evaluations may be discoverable. As with board evaluations, solicitor/client privilege is untested in this area and may not be upheld – even if the evaluation is conducted by a lawyer or an external facilitator retained through a law firm. It is therefore useful to consider practical ways to protect notes and other sensitive materials from this process. My own practice is to write all my interview notes in paper notebooks which can later be destroyed, create the reports on a USB drive, and avoid sending out individual director feedback reports on email, and only do so with pre-clearance from the Board Chair.

At the end of my individual feedback meetings, I typically give each director a paper copy of the feedback report so they can review it and digest some of the comments; with Zoom meetings, reports can be screen shared on-line, and hard copies sent afterwards.

It may be useful for the board to implement a policy requiring directors to shred the final paper report after it has served its purpose – even though this might be difficult to enforce in practical terms. Hard copies of board evaluation reports can easily be collected and destroyed at the end of the board meeting where they are discussed, particularly if this is an in-person meeting. Director evaluation reports, on the other hand, typically end up in board members' homes and offices.

> **Don't bother with an Action Plan.** An Action Plan is an essential final step in a board evaluation. But what matters most in a director evaluation is delivering constructive, actionable feedback to the recipients. Directors have a pretty good idea what they need to do once they've had a chance to review and discuss their feedback. And these steps seldom involve courses or coaching; it's nearly always about specific behaviors that most people know exactly how to fix, if they want to – whether this involves greater attentiveness in board meetings, making an effort to keep questions at an oversight level, avoiding entrenched positions, or any number of other modifications or initiatives, depending entirely upon the feedback received.

As we review the feedback report, directors often kick around ideas about how best to address these issues and we brainstorm on that. However, I have seldom found much value in memorializing these conclusions in an Action Plan – and believe that most directors would find this tactic somewhat off-putting, even a bit patronizing.

Frequency and Prevalence

There is no need to conduct director evaluations annually. As with board evaluations, a comprehensive process of this nature is overkill every year; every three years seems to be the optimal frequency. Some boards with staggered terms conduct director evaluations for each director in the year their term is expiring; the director evaluation is then factored into the re-nomination decision. As most staggered terms run for three years, the three-year cycle works here as well, albeit in a slightly different format. One board that I worked with several years ago adopted this three-year cycle: Board Evaluation in Year One; Committee Evaluations in Year Two, and Director Evaluations in Year Three.

According to the *U.S. Spencer Stuart Board Index*,[20] some 44% of S&P500 boards now conduct director evaluations – an increase from 38% the prior year, with prevalence having doubled (from 22%) over the past decade. At this pace, Spencer Stuart's research suggests director evaluations will likely become a majority practice among the S&P500 within the next three years. The 2020 PwC directors survey noted that director evaluations are even more important "as boards face the unique challenges of 2020" and concluded: "For boards that are not yet conducting individual performance assessments of each director, now is the time to institute the practice."[21]

However, even those boards that have adopted individual director assessments may need to rethink and redesign them. Given that half the PwC respondents for two years in a row believe that at least one of their fellow directors needs to be replaced it's apparent that some of these assessment processes either need to be redesigned or board leadership needs to step up more effectively in using them. Moreover, nearly 20% of directors in the 2020 PwC study expressed the view that their director evaluation process is ineffective.[22]

Chair Evaluations

Board leadership is one of the eight key parameters of board-building, as outlined in Appendix A. For this reason, questions around this topic should always be incorporated into a board evaluation. These questions should be tailored to reflect each board's circumstances – and every board is different in terms of the issues that might need to be explored: The Chair may be outstanding, but there's clearly no one on the board to succeed them. The Chair/CEO roles may be combined – and people wish the Lead Director would step up more in agenda design and meeting facilitation. The Chair and CEO may have an acrimonious relationship. Or a relationship that seems far too cozy – nobody feels confident that the Chair will challenge the CEO or deliver "bad news" from the executive sessions.

Feedback around these issues is nearly always surfaced during a board evaluation and addressed in the board evaluation report. However, where there are some particularly contentious issues or where there is just a lot of rich feedback that seems out of place in the board evaluation report, my practice has typically been to prepare an individual report for the Board Chair along the lines of a director evaluation. I'm up front with the board members when I do this – as they have been forthright and open in sharing their views and I want them to know that these issues are being addressed with the Chair directly even if they are not included in the board evaluation report. Sometimes a similar report is created for the CEO, as in scenarios where the CEO's working relationship with the board is significantly impacting the board's overall effectiveness.

During an individual director evaluation process, a broader range of feedback is typically elicited for the Board Chair and/or Lead Director than for other directors. It is essential to cover not only the Chair's most important strengths and advice for potential improvement but also to ensure that commentary is elicited relative to all key facets of the Chair's role:

- **Meeting facilitation**: Is the Chair an effective meeting facilitator? Do they draw out different perspectives from around the board table on critical issues? Or dominate the meetings and insist on driving home their point of view? Does the Chair intervene when directors delve into micro-management or go off on tangents?

---

20 Spencer Stuart, 2019 *U. S. Spencer Stuart Board Index* (October, 2019). Accessed September 29, 2020 at www.spencerstuart.com/research-and-insight/us-board-index.

21 PwC, "Turning Crisis into Opportunity", 15.

22 Ibid, 14.

Are they able to drive board consensus and give clear direction to management when a board decision is reached?

- **Working Relationship with the CEO**: Is there evident mutual respect between these two leaders? Or does their relationship seem tense and troubled? Or far too cozy – even suffocating? Is the Chair able to deliver tough messages from the board to the CEO and deal with CEO performance issues effectively? If the CEO is new in their role, is the Chair serving as an effective mentor, fostering a constructive working relationship between the CEO and the board? Or have they largely ignored the new CEO now that the succession process has been completed?

- **Working Relationship with the Board:** Does the Chair keep "a finger on the pulse" of the board through regular contact with directors between meetings to see what's on their minds? Do they make efforts to build relationships with all members of the board – or only with a "select few"? Does the Chair respect director confidences – or are board members guarded in sharing their views, fearing that they'll soon be repeated with attribution? Does the Chair step up and address thorny issues of director performance – or simply turn a blind eye?

- **Ambassadorial Role/Special Assignments:** Some Chairs play an important ambassadorial role, representing the company within the community, with employees, with major shareholders and in other ways. If this is an essential facet of the Chair's role, it also should be addressed. If the Chair played an important role in CEO succession/selection, led a special board committee, or took a primary role in dealing with a shareholder activist, questions should also be incorporated in this regard.

I've been privileged. Most of the Board Chairs/Lead Directors I've worked with have been champions. That's not surprising. Champions want to build and lead outstanding boards, so they value external resources who can help them to achieve that goal. Any Board Chair/Lead Director that's a true champion will typically embrace the idea of getting constructive feedback. In fact, these leaders – who often get amazing feedback that underscores their many strengths and contributions – will almost inevitably say, "That's all nice, but let's cut to the chase: What can I do better?"

But what if your Board Chair/Lead Director is not a champion? What if they are a preservationist? Preservationist Chairs are terrified by the idea of evaluations, especially if they're cognizant of their shortcomings as a board leader. The last thing they want is to have these issues spill out and force them to step down from the role they love, Chair of the Board. I don't think I've ever been hired by a preservationist Chair. But I've certainly run into a good number of them over the past two decades – and in some of these instances I **have** been asked to provide feedback on their leadership, either as part of a board or director evaluation process. I was nearly always hired in this regard by the Chair of the Governance Committee, who had carriage of board and director evaluations – and who was a boardroom champion.

Interestingly, despite strong initial reservations, the vast majority of the preservationist Chairs/Lead Directors who found themselves participating in these processes respected the feedback, because it was presented in a constructive, actionable way. They immediately understood where they needed to improve. They didn't like it, but many of them stepped up and tried to do better.

Some resigned. Two of the instances referenced earlier where directors resigned right in their interviews involved Board Chairs. Three other Chairs resigned shortly after receiving their feedback. A few Chairs (okay, one was a Lead Director) resigned about a year later. Interestingly, there was one instance in which the Chair resigned but the board interceded: They agreed that he should step down as Board Chair – he was a poor meeting facilitator who was clearly intimidated by the company's new CEO. But they didn't feel he should leave the board altogether; he stayed on as a regular board member.

And yes, on two occasions, I have been fired by a Board Chair who didn't like their feedback. It happens.

Director Expectations

Many boards develop Director Expectations. These serve to clarify what is expected of board members and can be useful in both director recruitment and director performance management. If a Director Expectations exercise is conducted in the right way, it can also create some positive changes in both board dynamics, director performance, and the board/management relationship.

Here's how it works: During the board evaluation, respondents are asked: "What are your expectations of the people who serve on this Board of Directors?" This is not a "test" around the role of the board where the interviewees are expected to rhyme off comments about fiduciary duties and the business judgment rule. This is about appropriate expectations of board members in fulfilling their responsibilities. Typical responses involve effort, commitment, and mutual respect. It can also be useful to ask questions regarding expectations of management: "What do you feel the board can and should expect from the CEO and the management team? What does the board need from management in order to fulfill its responsibilities?" And of course, "What are your expectations of the Board Chair?"

Probing is frequently required to flesh out the responses. But in the end, there is nearly always enough consensus to create a working draft of Director Expectations along the lines of the sample found in Appendix E-1, which is then discussed with the full board. Expectations of Management in Working with the Board (see sample in Appendix E-2) are typically discussed either in a joint session with the board and management or a meeting of the executive team (often attended by the Board Chair, Lead Director or Governance Committee Chair) and finalized thereafter. Sample Expectations of the Board Chair are found at Appendix E-3.

This is a far different process than the old self-assessment ploy where directors would rate themselves against a list of questions, like "I arrive at meetings well-prepared." The difference lies in the fact that this process engages every director – and typically management as well – in the development of the Expectations. This is the reason why positive changes frequently result: Board members who've become casual about reviewing their board books may start spending more time on meeting preparation. Those who've been weighing in on every agenda item may pick their spots more carefully.

But without that level of engagement in developing the Expectations, the exercise has little impact. For example, someone might think that a clever shortcut could involve simply recrafting Appendices E-1, E-2, and E-3 for application to their own board. After all, Expectations are not much different from board to board. But that misses the point: The whole reason this exercise works is that *every* member of the board weighs in on these issues, expresses their views, and the whole board discusses the results. This is what creates buy-in, which the mere circulating of a draft can ever achieve.

Director Expectations are not a replacement for individual director evaluations. This exercise will never create the kind of improvement that constructive individual director feedback can achieve. Nor does it serve to effectively put any underperforming directors "on notice" relative to re-nomination decisions. But in situations where the board lacks the funds – or the appetite – to undertake a director evaluation process, a Director Expectations exercise might be something to consider.

New Director 360

This is a director evaluation process specifically designed to provide new board members with practical feedback about 12–18 months into their tenure. The concept emerged from a client project involving some very sophisticated new directors with extensive board experience. The Governance Chair wanted to upgrade the board's director evaluation process to make it more valuable for directors of this caliber.

Appendix F provides a sample of a New Director 360 Feedback Report, which is more comprehensive than a typical director evaluation report because of the expanded range of interviewees. The New Director 360 involves interviews not only with other members of the board, but also with senior executives who regularly attend board and committee meetings as well as the board's external auditors and compensation consultants.

A New Director 360 exercise can serve three important functions:

i.   **It reinforces where the new director has already made strong contributions:** Receiving positive and specific feedback from the rest of the board is especially meaningful to new directors. It reinforces what they're doing well and lets them know their efforts have been appreciated. Actual examples in the comments that describe instances where a new director has made a particularly insightful or important contribution are valued far more than generic remarks like, "You've been a really great addition to our board", which is typically all that new directors get without a structured process like this one.

ii. **It nips any problems in the bud.** Some directors do get off to a rocky start – and it's much easier to address those problems early on. Early in their tenure, board members are particularly appreciative of constructive feedback alerting them to areas where they might do well to change their approach. And again, specificity is key – this is what enables a new board member to take some appropriate action and resolve the situation; vague, general comments such as "Things don't seem to be going as well as we had hoped" aren't helpful at all.

iii. **It offers well-considered recommendations for continued director development.** One of the unique facets of a New Director 360 is that it has both an evaluative *and* a developmental focus. Interviewees are asked for suggestions for the new director(s) to consider in continuing their development. Sometimes this involves innovative ideas to learn more about the company's business or industry. Other comments may focus on how the new director could best leverage their subject matter expertise. These can range from visits to a particular company site ("As Rachel is not from our industry, I think she'd do well to visit the shipyard in Los Angeles; I know that's what gave me a real feel for our logistics issues.") to meetings with specific employees ("Jack is a tech guru and it would be awesome if he'd have coffee one day with the people on the new digital team; I am sure they would love that – and it would give Jack more insights about what we're doing in this area than he'd ever pick up in a board meeting").

The New Director 360 is a new process in the world of director evaluations – and one with tremendous potential. Even a board that has yet to incorporate director evaluations into its governance process may nonetheless find it valuable to use a New Director 360 as the final component of the board's Director Orientation Program.

In Summary.........

Director performance management is not something most boards do well; many only consider director evaluations when they want to address an issue with a "problem director". While they can certainly be used effectively in these scenarios, director evaluations should never be merely a trap for underperforming board members. Providing constructive, actionable feedback that is genuinely worthwhile to *all* directors is essential in building an effective governance team. It also underscores the board's commitment to accountability and performance, setting the right "tone at the top."

This chapter lays out the key components of a genuinely worthwhile director evaluation process. It's important to design the process so as to elicit specific, constructive and balanced feedback. Walking through the feedback to discuss and answer questions is essential – but Action Plans are not.

The New Director 360 is a recent innovation designed for directors who have served on the board 12–18 months, which includes both evaluative and developmental components. It reinforces strengths, nips problems in the bud, and offers practical suggestions for continued director development – a worthwhile consideration as the capstone to an effective Director Orientation Program, even for boards that don't conduct director evaluations on a regular basis.

APPENDICES

Appendix A: Eight Key Parameters of Board-Building

There are eight key factors in board-building – all of which need to be optimized for any board to function at the top of its game. Board composition is the most important of the eight. In fact, pulling all the other seven levers will achieve only marginal results if the board has the wrong make-up to begin with. That said, a board that boasts a team of outstanding and diverse directors whose expertise aligns beautifully with the company's business model and strategic direction will never maximize the board's effectiveness unless and until the other seven parameters of board effectiveness are optimized as well. In fact, they will under-utilize and waste the talent at their board table.

An effective board evaluation should explore all eight parameters of board effectiveness. However, the protocol should be tailored to go into more depth on issues that are particularly timely and important to the board at the time of the evaluation so as to derive the greatest value from the evaluation process, rather than simply using a "cookie cutter" board evaluation template. For example, if the board is considering forming a Risk Committee, questions should be included about board committee structure, the goals and mandates of the new Risk Committee etc. Similarly, if the Chair is 1-2 years away from retirement, exploring issues around criteria for the board's next Chair, the process to select a new Chair, keeping the Chair independent versus combining the role with that of the CEO may all be useful topics to incorporate into the board evaluation interviews.

Graphic 1: Eight Key Parameters of Board Effectiveness

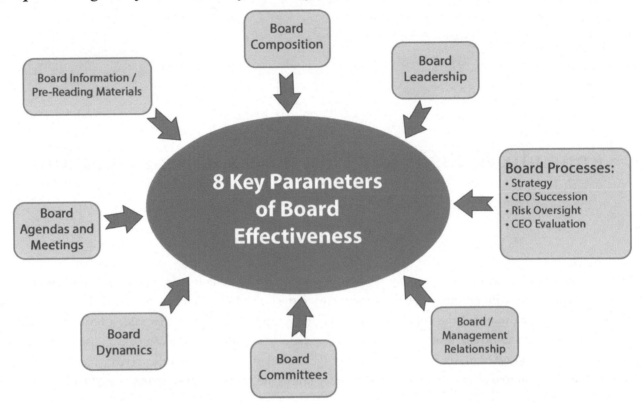

- **Board Composition:** Do the skills, experience and backgrounds of the people gathered at your board table make sense within the context of the company's business model and strategy? Are there evident gaps in the board's make-up – skills/background that would make a real difference to include in your board debates? Has there been a hesitancy to add them because you're waiting for upcoming retirements? Is diversity an issue: Few if any female or minority directors, a balance of active vs retired directors, board members that bring an international perspective if this is a factor in the company's growth strategy? Is the process for recruiting director candidates effective? What kind of orientation do new directors receive to get them quickly up the learning curve of the company's business?

- **Board Information/Pre-Reading Materials**: Many boards today are overloaded with data – typically a myriad of financial data – that is often poorly organized and fails to highlight the key points directors need to focus their attention on. The quality of board discussion and decision-making is directly proportionate to the quality of information the board receives. Even if the information is all there – somewhere – failing to organize it succinctly undercuts the value of assembling it in the first place. Some board packages have followed the same format for years. While board portals have become almost universal, a change in the delivery vehicle doesn't address fundamental shortcomings of the content of the information itself.

- **Board Agendas and Meetings**: Many boards have used the same agenda format for years – without standing back to consider whether the board meetings would be more effective if they were structured somewhat differently. What is the balance of presentation vs. discussion time in board meetings? If the balance is roughly 75% presentation and 25% discussion, the board is primarily being used as an audience rather than a thought-partner, a waste of directors' talent and expertise. Are critical issues placed near the front of the agenda – so that they can be tackled while directors are fresh and keen to engage? Or is that prime slot filled up with compliance issues and committee updates? Do agenda items regularly run over their allotted time – and if so, is this due to poor agenda design or poor meeting management?

- **Board Leadership:** How effective is the Chair in running the board meetings? Do they draw out different perspectives from around the table on key issues? Or does the Chair insist on driving their point home to the exclusion of other views that may be suppressed by this style? Do they know when to call the question on an issue and move on? Or is the board routinely going off on tangents? Is the Chair able to drive the board to consensus and give clear direction to management when a board decision is reached? Whether the independent board leader is a Non-Executive Chair or Lead/Presiding Director: How effective is this individual in working with the CEO and with the other directors? Do they keep a finger on the pulse of the board through regular contact between meetings? Are director confidences respected? Is the Chair willing to address thorny issues of director performance or do they simply turn a blind eye?

- **Board Committees:** The question here is seldom whether the committee is complying with the terms of its charter but rather, how effectively the committee is functioning. Does the Committee Chair run effective meetings and bring the committee to consensus? What about the quality and organization of committee pre-reading materials? Does the committee get effective support from company executives and external advisors? How are non-committee members kept abreast of the committee's work and decision-making? Should the board form a new committee and if so, what would be its mandate? Or should it disband an existing committee that is not required by regulations and has outlived its usefulness?

- **Board Dynamics:** What is the climate of this boardroom: Is it relatively uninspiring or a vibrant, energized place to exchange ideas and make decisions? Are board members candid or cautious in expressing their views? Has the board become polarized, either through a merger or different generations of directors, which have created "camps"? Many boards describe their culture as "collegial" – but does that denote an atmosphere of healthy mutual respect or a clubbiness characterized by "group think"? Can board members handle conflict and strong differences of opinion? Are challenges and different points of view encouraged or largely suppressed? Do people say what they think in the meetings – or out in the hall, afterwards?

- **Board/Management Relationship:** Is the relationship between the board and management characterized by candor and mutual respect or do board members take a high-handed manner with company executives? Is management comfortable sharing bad news and tough issues? Or is the board quick to criticize any missteps or risks that didn't pan out? Does management truly use the board as a thought partner to wrestle with critical issues? Or is everything presented to the board fairly "buttoned up" with the hope that questions will be minimal? Is management open to the board's advice or do they immediately become defensive? Has the board fallen into habits of micro-management, delving into picayune levels of detail that not only wastes board time but leaves company executives constantly feeling "second guessed"?

- **Board Processes:** This refers to the way the board engages in some of its most critical areas of oversight and decision making, including corporate strategy, risk, CEO succession planning, and CEO evaluation. Strategy and succession are both critical areas of board responsibility – and one of these two tends to arise as an area for improvement in nearly every board evaluation. Risk oversight in the aftermath of COVID-19 is a critical governance issue. Most CEOs find their annual evaluation process less than inspiring; some CEO evaluations involve board members rating the CEO on aspects of performance that they have little basis to judge, such as the CEO's communications within the company. Many boards that have the other seven parameters of board effectiveness in very good shape fall short in the area of board processes – perhaps ironic because, of all eight parameters, this is the area where an effective board can often make its most significant contributions to the company it governs.

Appendix B-1: Sample Board Evaluation Action Plan

This Action Plan summarizes key outcomes from the XYZ board evaluation and the discussion of the findings at the October 10, 2018 board meeting. It is intended primarily as a roadmap for the Board to use over the next 12–18 months in implementing action items developed from the board evaluation discussion so as to keep these initiatives on track.

Topic	Activity	Responsibility	Target Date
Board Pre-Reading	Changes to be implemented in board pre-reading papers: • **Implementation of executive summaries that outline the business case for key agenda items and proposals in 1–3 pages** • **Appendix of "additional documents" (non-essential but interesting documents that used to be included in the pre-reading) as a link from which board members can select those, if any, they wish to see or receive** • **Ongoing work to further streamline and improve board papers (elimination of industry acronyms, jargon, etc.)**	Corporate Secretary working with the Chairman, CEO, and executive team	Some changes to be implemented by December 15, 2018 meeting; others over the next 6 months
	Board pre-reading papers to be provided to directors 5 days in advance of board meetings (other than in exceptional circumstances)	CEO and Corporate Secretary	December 15, 2018 meeting and ongoing
	Board agenda item to review changes made to board pre-reading and discuss further improvements, if any	Chairman and Corporate Secretary; Full Board	July 12, 2019 meeting
CEO Sucession Planning	Discussion and development of criteria for XYZ's next CEO and development of draft timeline of key steps in the CEO succession planning process that reflect: • **Timeline and key steps for successor development (internal successor), including significant apprenticeship period with the current CEO** • **Decision timeline and key steps for successor development (external successor), including a worldwide executive search**	Chairman and HR Committee in collaboration with CEO	Discussion by HR Committee at December/18, February 3 and April 6/19 committee meetings Discussion with full board at July 12/19 board meeting

Executive Succession Planning	Review of executive talent pipeline/bench strength readiness for key executive positions (including Presidents of Subsidiaries) with CEO and CHRO	Chairman, HR Committee, CEO and CHRO	Review by HR Committee at April 6/19 meeting; review with full board at July 12/19 board meeting
Board Meetings	Efforts made to streamline Committee Chair updates by limiting these updates to 2 highlights slides	Committee Chairs; Chairman	December 15/18 board meeting; ongoing thereafter

Appendix B-2: Sample Board Evaluation Action Plan

Director Recruitment	❖ To recruit at least 2 new board members by year-end who collectively bring the following skills/expertise to the ABC board table: • **Board leadership experience/potential** • **Industry experience** • **International/Global Business experience** • **Technology experience/background** ***Primary Responsibility:*** Nominating and Governance Committee ***Timeline:*** By December 31, 2019
Board Meeting Management	❖ Develop and implement the use of an Annual Board Calendar that incorporates all main topics/regulatory compliance requirements for ABC Corporation throughout the year ***Primary Responsibility***: General Counsel ***Timeline***: Developed and finalized by July 1, 2019 ❖ Incorporate Chairman's letter at the start of each board meeting package ***Primary Responsibility***: Chairman ***Timeline:*** Already incorporated into July 14, 2019 package; ongoing ❖ Management Run-Through's Prior to Board meetings for the rest of 2019 ***Primary Responsibility:*** CHRO (working with CEO and GC) ***Timeline:*** Already underway ❖ One board meeting each year to be held at an ABC manufacturing facility ***Primary Responsibility:*** CEO ***Timeline:*** Incorporated into Annual Board Calendar. First off-site board meeting to be held before December 31, 2019

Board Pre-Reading Materials	❖ Development of executive summaries for each package of materials (1–2 pages max) relating to a board agenda item that reflects (i) Objectives for the board presentation; (ii) 3–4 critical things the board needs to know about this subject, including red flags – items of greatest concern/risk; and (iii) 2–3 key dilemmas this issue presents ***Primary Responsibility:*** CEO, GC, CHRO – coordinating with all management presenters ***Timeline:*** To commence at the July 14, 2019 board meeting; ongoing
Board Leadership	❖ Chairman to initiate annual conversations with each director – one-on-one meetings with no agenda held over a lunch/dinner for a wide-ranging discussion of board and corporate issues ***Primary Responsibility***: Chairman ***Timeline:*** Conversations to be scheduled and held throughout 2019. All should be completed by December 31, 2019. If considered worthwhile, this will become an ongoing annual process
CEO and Executive Succession Planning	❖ Develop a Long-Term CEO succession planning framework that includes: • **Annual talent reviews (1/2 day by the HR Committee)** • **Assessment of internal candidates relative to CEO profile and creation of development plans** • **Bench strength analysis** • **External talent review** ***Primary Responsibility:*** Chair of the HR Committee ***Timeline:*** To be completed by December 31, 2019
Director On-Boarding Program	❖ Add more structure to the current director on-boarding program consistent with the recommendations on page 10 of the Board Evaluation Report ***Primary Responsibility:*** General Counsel, CHRO ***Timeline:*** Program to be redesigned by Sept 1, 2019 so it can be used with new board recruits in the second half of 2019 and/or early 2020

Appendix C: Sample Excerpts – Board Benchmarking Reports

(i) Sample Board Composition Analysis: Primary Expertise/Skills/Background

	Corporate CEO/COO	Finance	Industry Expertise	Info Technology	Political	Academic Institution	Marketing	Legal	Other	TOTAL Outside Directors
Company A	5 (36%)	4 (29%)	3 (21%)			1 (7%)		1 (7%)		14 (100%)
Company B		1 (14%)	3 (43%)			1 (14%)	1 (14%)	1 (14%)		7 (100%)
Company C	1 (8%)	4 (31%)	4 (31%)	1 (8%)				1 (8%)	2 (15%)	13 (100%)
Company D	1 (8%)	2 (17%)	6 (50%)	3 (25%)						12 (100%)
Company E	4 (36%)	2 (18%)	2 (18%)	2 (18%)	1 (9%)					11 (100%)
Company F	4 (50%)	1 (12%)	2 (25%)	1 (12%)						8 (100%)
Company G	5 (50%)	2 (20%)	1 (10%)	1 (10%)			1 (10%)			10 (100%)
Company H	3 (33%)	1 (11%)	1 (11%)	2 (22%)			1 (11%)		1 (11%)	9 (100%)
Company I		3 (38%)	2 (25%)		2 (25%)			1 (12%)		8 (100%)
Company J		4 (44%)	2 (22%)	2 (22%)				1 (11%)		9 (100%)
Company K	5 (42%)	1 (8%)		2 (17%)	2 (17%)		1 (8%)		1 (8%)	12 (100%)

NOTE: For the purpose of this analysis, directors were included in only one rather than multiple categories based on the analyst's best judgment as to the primary reason for the director's appointment to arrive at 100% for "all categories". For example, where one director was a CEO with industry experience, it has been assumed that this individual's recruitment primarily related to his/her industry background. The CEO/COO category includes only board members with CEO/COO backgrounds from other industries.

(ii) Sample Board Composition Analysis: Diversity

	Gender		Ethnicity		
	% Female	# of Female Directors	% Ethnic Minorities	# of Ethnic Minority Directors	TOTAL Board Size
Company A	20%	3	0.7%	1- African American	15
Company B	38%	3	25%	1- African American 1- Hispanic	8
Company C	29%	4	43%	3- African American 1- Asian American 2- Hispanic	14
Company D	46%	6	46%	3- African American 3- Asian American	13
Company E	33%	4	0.8%	1- Hispanic	12
Company F	22%	2	22%	1- African American 1- Hispanic	9
Company G	27%	3	18%	1- African American 1- Hispanic	11
Company H	10%	1	20%	1- African American 1- Asian American	10
Company I	10%	1	0%		10
Company J	10%	1	20%	1- African American 1- Hispanic	10
Company K	29%	4	43%	3- African American 2- Asian/Asian American 1- Hispanic	14

(iii) Sample Board Composition Analysis: Board Experience

	Public Company	Private Company	Foundation, Charitable, or Other Non-Profit	Academic Institution	Government Entity Board	Other	TOTAL # of Outside Directors with Some Board Experience
Company A	3 (21%)	2 (14%)	3 (21%)	7 (50%)	1 (7%)	1 (7%)	11/14 (79%)
Company B			3 (43%)			1 (14%)	3/7 (43%)
Company C	6 (46%)	3 (23%)	6 (46%)	3 (23%)	1 (8%)		11/13 (85%)
Company D	2 (17%)	2 (17%)	4 (33%)			1(8%)	6/12 (50%)
Company E	9 (82%)	5 (45%)	4 (36%)			2 (18%)	11/11 (100%)
Company F	6 (75%)	2 (25%)	3 (38%)	4 (50%)		2 (25%)	8/8 (100%)
Company G	9 (90%)	2 (20%)	3 (30%)				10/10 (100%)
Company H	6 (67%)	3 (33%)	3 (33%)				8/ 9 (89%)
Company I	2 (25%)	3 (38%)	2 (25%)	1 (1%)		1(12%)	6/ 8 (75%)
Company J	7 (78%)	3 (33%)	3 (33%)		1 (11%)		9/ 9 (100%)
Company K	11 (92%)		3 (25%)	2 (17%)	2 (17%)		11/12 (92%)

(iv) Sample Board Policy Analysis – Director Retirement Policies

	Retirement Age	Retirement Policy
Company A	72	No director can stand for election after reaching age 72
Company B	70	Board Members must step down at the first Annual Meeting after they reach age 70.
Company C	72	No director can stand for election after reaching age 72. However, the full board has discretion to grant a waiver of this policy. (Note: In 2018, two directors age 73 were re-nominated to the board.)
Company D	70	A Board Member must resign at the first Annual Meeting that is held after the Member reaches age 70. The Governance Committee has discretion on this issue and may extend a Board Member's tenure beyond the age of 70 in appropriate circumstances.
Company E	72	No explicit retirement policy was found in Company E's governance materials. However, one of their directors who will turn 72 in 2019 is noted to be retiring mid-year, suggesting that Company E does in fact, have a retirement policy at age 72.
Company F	72	No director can serve a new term after reaching the age of 72. (This board has 3–year terms.)
Company G	70	No director can stand for election after reaching age 70, unless the board determines otherwise.
Company H	72	Directors must retire at age 72 at the Annual Meeting which coincides with the expiration of their annual term.
Company I	73	Directors are required to retire from the board at the Annual Meeting next following their 73rd birthday. The board may waive this requirement if it deems such waiver in the best interests of the company. (Note: Wm. Stone, Company I's former Chairman/CEO, age 73 was re-elected to the board in 2018.)
Company K	70	Absent exceptional circumstances agreed to by the majority of the board (excluding the affected member) each Board Member will resign upon reaching the age of 70 immediately at the next board meeting.

Appendix D-1

Sample Individual Director Feedback Report

Prepared for: Mike Smith

This individual director feedback report has been compiled to reflect themes and sample comments (*in italics*) from the individual director evaluation component of the 2018 board evaluation for ABC Biotech Ltd. ("ABC"). Themes presented herein were derived from an analysis of the feedback from interviews conducted between October 16 to November 18, 2018 with each member of the board. Directors were asked to consider both the individual strengths and contributions of each of their fellow board members and to offer advice or identify any areas for improvement that could further enhance each director's contribution to the board. Directors were both candid and thoughtful in this component of the interviews, offering direct and constructive feedback to their colleagues for their consideration.

For the CEO, Greg James, board members were asked to focus their feedback on Greg's working relationship with the Board, as this process is not intended as a CEO evaluation.

Major Strengths/Contributions

Mike is admired for his brilliant mind, genuine passion for the company, and depth of knowledge of the industry and its players. He thinks big and has confidence in the company, which emboldens management.

- *"Mike is absolutely indispensable in terms of his confidence in ABC. He thinks big. And that gives management confidence. After the IPO, Mike said, "This will become a very big company" – and said it with real assurance. People needed to hear that. That confidence had a very positive impact that I cannot overstate."*

- *"Mike has genuine passion for ABC and its science – and it shows. His commitment to and belief in the company are evident. Mike sees the stock as precious and sees the company as having a great future. Greg and his team have taken some bold steps over the past year, which have all worked out well; I think Mike has been a very positive influence in that regard."*

- *"Mike knows all the players in the biotech space, and he understands the key issues impacting the industry. He also really knows what investors are after. He has a brilliant mind and a genuine desire for ABC to succeed and be successful. He wants ABC to change the world and he believes that we can do it. That kind of spirit is incredibly valuable at our board table."*

- *"Mike has a vision for ABC; he believes in the company's science and knows we can make a difference in many peoples' lives. Mike also has great strategic acumen and a deep knowledge of the biotech industry. That's a powerful combination– and these are significant strengths. It is very rare to see a director with this level of passion for a company when he/she is not a founder and I really applaud that."*

Mike comes to board and committee meetings extremely well-prepared. His comments are insightful and nearly always bring a fresh perspective to the issue at hand.

- *"You can tell that Mike has put a lot of time into advance preparation for the board meetings. What's more, when Mike weighs in on an issue, I nearly always find myself saying, "Wow! That's a great point. I never thought of that." I think he is one of our most thoughtful directors and probably adds the most in terms of bringing different perspectives to our board discussions."*

- *"It's very evident that Mike has done a considerable amount of analysis before we get into the board meetings – particularly on the data relative to the science and the financial projections. Because of this, he makes extremely valuable contributions to the board discussions – and you can tell that the other board members genuinely value his insights."*

- *"Mike is a hard-working director who really does his homework prior to our meetings; that's very evident. What's more, he doesn't weigh in on every issue. When Mike has something to say, however, it's nearly always a new point no one has made before. He's not one of these guys that say, "Yes, I agree" and just eats up board time that way. When Mike speaks, he brings new perspectives to the fore – and that is a great strength that I wish other directors had."*

Advice/Areas for Improvement

Mike is advised to be a bit more mindful of how he's coming across to management in the meetings, particularly as he is held in very high regard. He may find it useful to think about the context of the room before making his comments – and reserve his more biting comments for executive sessions.

- *"Mike sometimes puts management down in the meetings and quarrels with other board members in front of management. That creates the appearance of strong board dissention. And that sort of thing goes to the employee coffee room in ten minutes. People hang on every word a director says – especially someone like Mike, who is held in extremely high regard. My advice to Mike would be to become a bit more mindful of who's in the room when he makes his comments. If it's a crappy presentation, we can shut it down and talk to Greg about it in the executive session afterwards. There is no need to put the management person down in front of their peers; I think that this reflects as badly on Mike as it does on the person he's critiquing."*

- *"Mike has dressed down management and shown disrespect for other directors at times. He needs to recognize that a boardroom is a fishbowl – management are watching and listening to the way he behaves. My best advice to Mike would be to consider the context of the room and hold his more biting comments until the executive sessions."*

- *"Mike takes a combative approach – but it comes from a well-intentioned place. Mike is a very smart guy who wants the company to succeed. And he does not suffer fools! My best advice to Mike would be to come across as more of a statesman and less of a warrior. Maybe not everyone on the management team is as smart as he is. But his job as a director is to give them advice and guide them to success. If they don't deliver, it's up to Greg to fire them. Mike can share his views with Greg off-line of the meeting; he doesn't need to go after executives in the board meeting. It is detracting from the very high regard in which he is held."*

Appendix D-2

Sample Individual Director Feedback Report

Prepared for: Roger White, Chair of the Compensation Committee

This report provides a summary of key themes from the director peer evaluation interviews conducted with all members of the Board of Directors of XYZ Corporation in October, 2018. Interview comments were summarized and analyzed, from which key themes were derived relative to each director's strengths, major contributions, and potential areas for further improvement. To provide directors with greater insights on each theme, sample interview comments are also provided in italics.

Major Strength

Roger is extremely articulate. He is readily able to synthesize ideas and effectively summarize key points, which board members find extremely valuable in their discussions and deliberations.

Related Comments from Peer Interviews:

- *"Roger is very articulate and expresses himself extremely well. At every nearly meeting, he'll find an opportunity to summarize a rather unwieldy board conversation in a way that brings closure to the issue. That's a real gift, and it really helps the board come to closure."*

- *"Roger is very organized in his thinking and very articulate. He's clearly thought about the issues in advance and has put time into considering how to address them in a thoughtful and structured way in the meetings."*

- *"Roger has an ability to take an issue and synthesize it down to a couple of crisp sentences. That's an ability that I don't have, and I really admire it in someone who has it."*

- *"Roger has very clear thinking and is able to put a tight spin on things. For example, Roger will summarize a conversation in the boardroom in a succinct way that really gets to the essence of it. His comments provide focus and when he makes them, I always find myself nodding and thinking, "Yes – that's it exactly. He nailed it!""*

Most Significant Contribution

Roger is viewed as having done a "masterful job" in chairing the Compensation Committee, which nearly all his peers highlighted as his most significant contribution to the board.

Related Comments from Peer Interviews:

- *"As Chair of the Compensation Committee, Roger picked up a real mess and straightened it out. Our compensation philosophy had no real rationale; it seemed to be a hodge-podge of different programs without an overarching focus in terms of what we were trying to accomplish with executive pay. Roger was able to bring order out of chaos, and I think now we are all very happy with where things stand on executive compensation."*

- *"The Compensation Committee is difficult to chair. Opinions run a wide spectrum and it can get emotional at times, especially on the part of management. Even when we decide on something, there continues to be a tenor of "second guessing" those decisions. I think Roger has done a masterful job of running that committee and overcoming many of these challenges."*

- *"Roger keeps in touch with what's happening not only in the compensation arena, generally, but in terms of what other companies in our industry are doing with their compensation programs. This has impressed me and under-scores Roger's level of commitment as Compensation Chair."*

- *"Roger has done a great job as the Chair of the Compensation Committee. He takes a very even-handed approach in chairing the committee – which is not always easy – and has been able to work extremely well with management on issues that are sometimes sensitive and emotional."*

Potential Areas for Enhancement

Roger comes so well-prepared for the Compensation Committee meetings that a wide-ranging discussion does not always ensue on important issues. This may be appropriate in many instances. However, on some of the more controversial issues, Roger may find it helpful to be aware of this and occasionally modify his style.

Related Comments from Peer Interviews:

- *"I realize there has been a lot of work done in advance of the Compensation Committee meeting by Roger, by the head of HR, by the compensation consultants, etc. But sometimes we're up for a discussion of an important issue but that discussion never materializes. It's all "baked" when it comes into the meeting. I don't feel we're having the level of broad dialogue on some compensation issues that we probably should be having, as a Committee."*

- *"Roger comes into the Compensation Committee with his mind made up about what needs to be accomplished – which is exactly what I expect in a good committee chair. However, he needs to focus on creating an atmosphere in his committee meetings that is more conducive to dialogue and discussion."*

- *"Roger needs to actively work at generating more discussion in the Compensation Committee."*

Appendix E-1

Sample Expectations of ABC Directors

The following DRAFT Expectations of the Board of Directors were developed from interviews held in December, 2017 with all ABC board members and members of ABC's management team who regularly interface with the board. This draft will be discussed at the Board Meeting scheduled for Jan. 28, 2018.

- **Preparation:** Prepare for board and committee meetings by reviewing the pre-reading materials in advance and reflecting on the key issues to be discussed. Come to the meetings ready to address the agenda items and get engaged in the discussions and debates.

- **Participation:** Actively participate in the board and committee meetings, drawing on your experience and expertise to bring relevant and constructive insights and perspectives into the board dialogue. Avoid dominating the board dialogue and/or speaking to "get your name in the minutes". Offer differing or contrary points of view, where appropriate.

- **Attentive:** Remain attentive and conscientious throughout board and committee meetings, avoiding the temptation to be distracted by electronic devices, etc.

- **Integrity/Confidentiality:** Always act with integrity and ethics. Focus on the best interests of ABC and its shareholders in board decision-making. Respect the confidentiality of board discussions and ABC business issues.

- **Avoid Micro-Management:** Focus your questions and comments at a governance/oversight level.

- **Say It in the Meeting:** Express your views in the meeting, not after the meeting is over.

- **Mutual Respect:** Engage with management and fellow directors in a respectful manner, even when making a counterpoint or expressing strong disagreement. Make an effort to build a constructive working relationship with fellow board members and members of the ABC management team.

- **Responsiveness:** Be responsive in replying to management requests and inquiries between meetings, wherever possible responding within 48 hours, even to acknowledge receipt of the request if it is not possible to attend to it within that time frame.

- **Keep Current:** Make an ongoing effort to keep abreast of developments in [ABC's industry], the global economy, key markets in regions where ABC does business and developments in public company governance. Make an effort to listen in to ABC's earnings calls with the financial analysts.

Appendix E-2

Sample Board Expectations of Management

The following DRAFT Expectations of the ABC Management Team in working with Board of Directors was developed from interviews held in December, 2017 with all ABC board members, and those members of ABC's management team who regularly interface with the board. This draft will be discussed at a joint session of the board and management to be held in conjunction with the Jan. 28, 2018 board meeting.

- **Leadership and Managerial Competence**: Run the company in a competent, businesslike way, providing leadership to the people who work at ABC to achieve strategic and financial goals.

- **Accountability**: Take responsibility for ABC performance and the achievement of corporate objectives; follow through on commitments.

- **Integrity:** Operate with ethics and integrity in running the company and in dealings with the Board.

- **Preparation**: Put effort into the pre-reading materials in preparation for Board and Committee meetings so as to make the best use of the board's time. Focus on the key issues, provide not just data and information but your insights into what the data means and the alternatives you have considered in making your recommendations to the Board.

- **Provide Industry Context**: Provide the board with information that enables directors to compare ABC with competitors in [ABC's industry] in terms of financial performance and other key metrics.

- **Provide Strategic Linkage**: Highlight the linkage between management proposals and ABC's strategic direction and strategic goals in preparing board materials and presentations.

- **Avoid Micro-Management**: Focus your pre-reading materials, board presentations, and discussions at a governance level; try to avoid dragging the board into management details.

- **Transparency/Mutual Respect**: Be candid in sharing your thinking with the board and in seeking their views on issues where they can be a true strategic thought partner to management. Don't get defensive if a board member asks a tough question or challenges your thinking.

- **Don't Surprise the Board**: Let the board know about important issues that are emerging – both potential problems and "big wins" – in a timely fashion.

Appendix E-3

SAMPLE Expectations of the Board Chair

The following DRAFT Expectations of the Board Chair of ABC were developed from interviews held in March, 2019 with all ABC board members

Establishes Clear Priorities Aligned with ABC's Strategic Objectives	At the start of each year, the Chair should establish clear board priorities and get alignment on these from the full board and the CEO. Priorities should be focused on ABC's strategic objectives; avoid the temptation to prioritize "pet issues".
Builds a Constructive Working Relationship with ABC's Chief Executive Officer	This relationship should be characterized by collaboration, mutual respect, candor, and effective ongoing communication.
Designs Effective Board Agendas	Develops agendas that focus on the most important issues facing ABC (consistent with the priorities mentioned above) and make the best use of board members' time.
Facilitates Effective Board Meetings	Keeps the board focused on agenda items and the discussion moving, drawing out different perspectives and encouraging participation. Able to steer board dialogue back to the agenda topic and/or to a governance level if it segues into unrelated items or micro-management. Able to bring the board to consensus on matters that require a decision.
Takes Responsibility for the Effectiveness of the Board, as a whole, and Director Performance Management	Focuses on optimizing the board's effectiveness throughout their tenure as Chair to achieve continuous improvement. Sets a high standard for board conduct by modeling performance expectations of directors in terms of commitment, mutual respect, and accountability. Intervenes, where necessary, if a director performance issue emerges.

Appendix F

Sample New Director 360: Individual Director Feedback Report

Prepared for Deborah Richards

Overview

This individual director feedback report has been compiled to reflect themes and sample comments (*in italics*) from the New Director 360 for Deborah Richards. This process involved a series of interviews with all members of the ABC Board of Directors, four members of the ABC executive team and a representative of Ernst & Young, ABC's external auditor. The interviews were conducted by Skype between Jan. 26 and Feb. 8, 2019.

Interviewees were asked to provide their views on Deborah's strengths and contributions as a new director of ABC based on their experience working with her over the past 12 months since she joined the board. They were also asked to offer advice or identify any areas for improvement that could further enhance Deborah's effectiveness and contributions to the ABC Board going forward. Over 100 individual comments were generated from the interviews. These have been summarized, analyzed. and grouped into key themes presented in this report.

Major Strengths/Contributions

Deborah's major strength, as the sitting Chief Financial Officer of a large global company, is clearly her wealth of expertise on a broad range of financial issues. She has already added tremendous value to Audit Committee discussions and in her meetings with internal audit (IA), where she served as a sounding board for the IA team on a broad range of issues. Most of Deborah's board colleagues cited her contributions to the board's discussions about changing ABC's dividend policy as one of her most significant contributions to date; Deborah drew on her experience to challenge ABC's long-standing views around this issue – and changed the board's thinking.

- *"We are extremely fortunate to have someone with Deborah's vast array of financial expertise at our board table. And the fact that she is a sitting CFO is really the "icing on the cake" because she is so current on the issues and brings such relevant and insightful perspectives. I particularly commend her for making the time to sit down with Internal Audit not only at her orientation session – which lasted two hours longer than it was supposed to – but also at another meeting a few months later. She spent time getting to know the people in IA and created a nice, informal environment where everyone was comfortable just kicking around some of the issues and getting the benefit of her wisdom and experience. It was invaluable."*

- *"Deborah has rejuvenated our Audit Committee. Everyone in those meetings – particularly our own IA team and even E&Y - are benefiting from her contributions. She backs them up, at times, and you can tell they appreciate that because she comes at these issues from a very solid knowledge base. She is also respectful of our Audit Chair – and I feel that's important to mention, as well. Deborah is clearly very conscious not to overstep and essentially 'take over the committee,' which she could easily do. That shows a lot of maturity and professionalism; it's something I've really admired about her."*

- *"The reason we recruited Deborah to the board was for her financial expertise – and she has already gone above and beyond in this domain. Her comments and questions, particularly in the Audit Committee, reflect her depth of knowledge and currency; she brings and draws on a wealth of experience and challenges the way we've viewed things in the past. Perhaps the most evident example of this relates to the board debate around the dividend where she encouraged the board to consider some different perspectives – and, as a result, we changed our policy. I also think it was Deborah's approach that made all the difference – clearly, she had wrestled with this issue personally, as a CFO, and could bring all of that to bear. But she offered her views in a generous way, by which I mean she didn't feel the need to make the people who held a different view "wrong" so that she could be "right".*

- *"When Deborah speaks – particularly on financial issues – people listen. In her first or second board meeting, an issue about our dividend came up and Deborah made some great points about the changing dynamics of our shareholder base. This was the kind of issue where a new director could get out on a limb and lose credibility, as she was challenging some longstanding views. But she triumphed! That was the moment that Deborah kind of 'earned her wings' with this board, and she hasn't looked back."*

- *"The dividend has been a sacred cow at this company for as long as I can remember. And Deborah took that bull by the horns – and changed the board's thinking. That, in my view, is her most significant contribution to date, but it's the most significant of many. Deborah is well on her way to becoming one of ABC's best directors, in my opinion."*

Deborah's contributions to discussions on M&A integration have also been particularly insightful – and notable because the most important of these related to corporate culture, rather than finance. This demonstrated Deborah's breadth as a director and prompted the board to engage in a critical debate that added significant value for the management team, leveraging, among other things, her own learnings from another M&A integration experience.

- *"One of the things our management team has really struggled with is M&A integration. Everybody wants to do the deal – but the integration piece hasn't always gone smoothly. This is an area where Deborah can and already has made major contributions – and interestingly, this was not related to finance. She spoke up about the cultural integration issues of the XYZ deal and explained, in very practical terms, how this became a huge obstacle in a deal she had worked on a few years back, which also involved the acquisition of a founder-controlled company. Everybody on the board was absolutely riveted when she described this and she brought up points that I don't think anyone else on the board – or in management – had even considered."*

- *"Deborah has had a long track record of doing M&A deals as a CFO and even before that. She understands deal structure, and she is particularly well-attuned to the issues involved in successful MA& integration, which is something we've struggled with in the past. Having the benefit of her insights in these discussions is incredibly valuable not only to the board, but also to the management team."*

- *"One thing that perhaps surprised me – because I tend to think of Deborah as a finance expert – is that she really gets 'people issues' too. This came to the fore in our discussions around the XYZ acquisition. She made some great points on financial issues involved in the deal – and I kind of expected that. But then she weighed in on the 'people issues' involved in integrating a founder-led company into a large public company, recounting her experience when 123 acquired 456. She described what she learned from this – and what 123 should have done differently. This opened up a terrific board discussion, and I think management walked out of that meeting saying, "Wow! That's what a good board does for a management team!" And we wouldn't have had that discussion, had Deborah not raised the points that she did."*

- *"Probably most people will say that Deborah's most significant contribution to the board to date involved the dividend issue. But I think it was the conversation she initiated around the integration of the XYZ deal. We tend to look at the deal financing and the projected synergies – but Deborah really got us to look 'under the covers' at some of the practical issues of trying to merge a proud, successful founder-led company into a F500 and that was one of the best board discussions I think we've had this year."*

Deborah clearly does her homework for board meetings and is extremely well-prepared. It's evident that she has not just read the materials but has given considerable thought to the issues at hand. She 'picks her spots' and tends to weigh in only where she has a different perspective or new angle on the topic, rather than simply reinforcing and building upon the comments of others.

- *"It's very apparent from the questions Deborah raises and the comments she makes in board meetings that she's not only read the board briefing materials, she's reflected on the issues and has taken some pains to try to think of an angle that we may not have considered. She also picks her spots; she doesn't weigh in on everything – when she dives into the board discussion, you know she's going to raise a new perspective that nobody else has mentioned – or probably even thought of. Every so often, the point she makes is a bit 'off the wall' – but that's fine; that's refreshing sometimes, and it doesn't happen much. Eight times out of ten, she's spot on and is making a big difference in terms of our discussion."*

- *"One of my biggest concerns when we were recruiting Deborah was whether she'd really commit the time to be on our board; after all, she's a sitting CFO at a large, global company. But any fears I may have had on that front have been long dispelled. Not only does she come well prepared, it's evident that she's really thought about the issues and has made some decisions about where she's going to weigh in, so as to try to add real value. That, in my view, is what a really top-notch director does, and she's already got it down cold."*

- *"There are two things that really drive me nuts in board meetings – and maybe they drive Deborah nuts too, as a CFO at her own company, because she is studiously avoiding both: The first is people who have clearly not read the board package – they waste everybody's time asking questions that were already covered in the briefings. Deborah would never dream of doing that; it's evident that she's read it all, and she's made notes. The second is people who take up a lot of board time agreeing with what someone else has said – rather than offering a different view. Sometimes I think these people just want to say something to get their name in the minutes. Well, that is certainly not Deborah's style and that is very much to her credit. When Deborah speaks up, she is nearly always injecting a fresh perspective or raising a point that no one else has mentioned. I think that's one of her most important strengths as a board member."*

Deborah's colleagues describe her as "warm, friendly and approachable"; they genuinely enjoy working with her. She's viewed as professional, respectful of others, a good team player, and a terrific role model for female executives.

- *"Deborah is a very warm person who's enjoyable to be with – and to work with. You get the sense that Deborah genuinely wants to contribute to the board as a team player, she's not someone who has to be a star. Now, in fairness, she's becoming a star and I think that's great – but she doesn't seem have a lot of ego in the room. She's respectful of everyone."*

- *"I think one of Deborah's strengths is that she's a good team player. She doesn't try to dominate the board discussion and you don't get the sense she's going to walk out the door in a huff if the board doesn't agree with her point of view; she's mature and professional."*

- *"The more I get to know Deborah, the better I like her. She's funny, warm, and inclusive – she brings people into conversations and makes a real effort to be part of the team. We could not have made a better choice than recruiting Deborah to become a member of our board, and we're extremely fortunate to have her."*

- *"I expected to be kind of intimidated by Deborah because hey – she's Deborah Richards, the CFO of 123 Corp. Well, I could not have been more pleasantly surprised! She's approachable and friendly –a really warm person who is very enjoyable to be with. She demonstrates respect for everyone – even the catering lady that comes into the board meetings. There is no better role model for our female executives than Deborah."*

Advice/Potential Areas for Improvement

The more that Deborah continues to learn about ABC's business and the unique facets of its industry, the more she can contribute. This is the area where her colleagues would encourage her to focus and made a number of constructive suggestions for her consideration, including site visits, discussions with operating executives below the C-suite, learning more about ABC's regulatory environment, attending an industry conference and/ or reading trade journals. As a sitting CFO, Deborah is extremely time-constrained – something her board colleagues recognize. They nonetheless believe that, if she can manage it, some further investment in her learning will yield tremendous benefits to Deborah, personally, and to the ABC board.

- *"Deborah is very time-constrained because she is a sitting CFO – and I recognize that. But she has the potential to become one of our best directors. Making that step to what I'll call 'the next level' in her board development will require Deborah to invest more time in learning about the operational side of ABC's business. She's a quick study and I don't think it will take that long. But she has no background in this industry and frankly, it shows in some of her comments. The more she understands the business context and the industry fundamentals, the greater her contributions will be. I'd encourage her – in the very strongest terms – to try to make some time for this. I believe it will yield significant benefits to her, personally, as well as to the board, in terms of her contributions."*

- *"I hate to even say this because Deborah has so much on her plate– but if I were going to give her any advice, it would be to invest the time it takes to learn more about the operational side of ABC's business. I don't think she's been to any of the plants, yet. And I know personally that just one or two site visits can give you a very different perspective – one site visit is worth a hundred PowerPoint slides! So, if I were her, I'd make that a priority. We run our operations 24/7 and if it's easier for her to go on a weekend, that's fine. We have a corporate jet – we'll pick her up and fly her there. We realize she's busy, and we need to make this easy for her. But it's something that we should try to arrange in the next few months."*

- *"I think the obvious advice to Deborah at this stage is to continue to learn about ABC's business. She's got the finance part down cold. And, as a director, she could just stay in that mode as one of the board's "finance experts" and still add a lot of value. But from what I've seen – especially some of her comments on M&A integration – Deborah has the potential to engage more broadly on strategic issues and really become someone who can guide this company's future. If she wants to make that leap – which I'd personally encourage her to do – then she needs to get a solid feel for this business and the critical factors in this industry: Who are the players and what are the global trends? What are the implications of our regulatory environment in practical terms? One 'quick and dirty' way to get up to speed is to go to the annual conference in Las Vegas – even for one day; that's a 'master class.' But if she can't find the time for that, then make an effort to read the trade journals, get out to the sites and try to spend time (even on a video conference) with some of the operating folks at the regional level."*

- *"Orientation is a 'drinking from a firehose' experience for most directors – and I'm sure it was for Deborah. Her Orientation was focused on finance – meetings with E&Y, the finance team, etc. The operational part of the business was kind of a 'flyover' - and that's where I'd encourage her to focus now. She has no background in this industry and there's a lot to learn. She's extremely smart and has picked up a lot already – but I'd encourage her to work with the GC to plan out an Orientation Part Two now that she's been on the board for a year. It shouldn't be a one-day thing – it should extend over the course of the year and respect her limited time. It could involve a couple of site visits, one now and another six months from now – an old plant and one of the new ones. I'd have her meet with some of the operations people and some of the regulatory people; she has never worked in an industry with this level of regulation. I know this will require a concerted effort on her part, but I'd look at it as an investment that will pay back huge dividends over the coming years."*

- *"When we recruited Deborah, she told us that she wanted the experience of serving on an outside board so that she could be a better CFO at her own company – and as professional development if she ever became a CEO. Having seen her in the boardroom, there is no doubt in my mind that a CEO role lies somewhere in her future. I think she can help herself achieve her development goals if she invests the time to learn more about ABC's business – so that she can become a true strategic partner of our CEO and our board rather than just "a finance specialist".*

- *"Deborah has earned a lot of fans on the board in the short time she's been with us. But what's getting in her way is the fact that she clearly doesn't understand certain facets of the business – and every so often she'll make a comment that underscores this and detracts from her credibility. What she needs to do is make an effort to continue to learn about the operational side of the business. You're not going to become an expert overnight – no one expects that! But if she organizes a few meetings with our top operational people as a sort of second phase of orientation, I think that would cover a lot of ground. She should also get out to the plants."*

- *"I think the obvious advice to Deborah, having only been on the board a year, is to continue her learning journey about ABC's business. But one piece of advice I'd mention in conjunction with that is: Part of what's been really terrific about Deborah's contributions to date is that she's challenged our thinking about how ABC does things. And I believe that the reason Deborah can offer fresh perspectives has something to do with the fact that she comes from a different industry. I don't want her to lose that! But I don't think she has to. Learning about ABC's business shouldn't mean that she can't continue to challenge its norms."*

At times, Deborah has allowed herself to become distracted by her electronic devices in board and Audit Committee meetings. While this temptation can be difficult to avoid – particularly for a sitting CFO – she would do well to become more cognizant of this issue and try to curtail it somewhat.

- *"Deborah is a terrific director, and I have no advice to give her other than to be a bit more mindful about what I'll call electronic distractions. She's constantly reading and returning emails during the Audit Committee meeting – maybe less at the board meeting, but I've seen it there too. I don't really think it's a case of not paying attention – all her questions are right on point. It's more the optics of this to the people presenting to the Committee."*

- *"Deborah is awesome! She is a fantastic addition to our board. She is so good that the one thing that drives me nuts is the fact that we never seem to have her full attention in the meetings, particularly the Audit Committee. She's fully present in the meeting one minute – and then she's focused on her iPhone. And really focused – like you can see in her face that something is going on that is not good and seems pretty urgent. And that distracts you too. You start to wonder, "Hmm … I wonder what's happening over at Deborah's company; must be some problem." And then you realize that you need to revert your own attention back to the Audit Committee. Is it a huge problem? No. Is it something she should try to curtail a bit? Probably, yes."*

- *"I serve on another board where we all have to place our phones into a box before we go into the board meeting. They implemented that policy because people were getting too distracted with emails during the meetings. I don't want to implement this sort of policy at ABC; people need their phones, they're a fact of modern life. I think it's far better to put people on notice that they're doing a bit too much phone-checking during the meetings – and they will stop. So, I guess I'm putting Deborah on notice: She needs to watch the amount of time she's spending on her iPhone during the meetings."*

- *"My only advice to Deborah can be summed up in four words: Turn off your iPhone. I realize she is a sitting CFO and she can't "go dark" on her own team for hours on end. But it's evident that she gets distracted by emails and texts during our board meetings – and frankly, she's such a good director that we want her full attention."*

- *"When the board meets, there is a row of chairs behind one side of the board table where some members of management sit during the meetings. The people sitting there can all see what is on the iPads of the board members sitting in front of them. And when they look at Deborah's iPad, they see that she is frequently checking the stock price of her own company and reading articles in the* Wall Street Journal. *In fairness, some peoples' presentations in our board meetings drone on and on – so, I really can't blame her. But she should try to limit that a bit."*

- *"Repeat after me: My name is Deborah, and I have an iPhone problem."*

References

Financial Reporting Council. *The UK Corporate Governance Code.* London: FRC. July, 2018.

Gregory, Holly J. "Rethinking Board Evaluation," *Practical Law: The Journal.* Chicago: Sidley Austin LLP. (March, 2015): 28–32.

Hodge, Chris. "The Hidden Cost of Board Meetings," London: Board Intelligence. May 17, 2018.

National Association of Corporate Directors. *Report of the NACD Blue Ribbon Commission on Culture as a Corporate Asset.* Arlington: NACD, 2017.

O'Hanley, Ronald and Rakhi Kuman. "Changing Board Practices and Culture to Meet Investor Expectations," *IQ Insights.* Boston: State Street Global Advisors. August, 2016.

PwC. "Insights from the Boardroom", *PwC's Annual Corporate Directors Survey.* New York: PwC. October, 2012.

———. "The collegiality conundum: Finding balance in the boardroom", *PwC's Annual Corporate Directors Survey.* New York: PwC, October 2019.

———. "Turning crisis into opportunity", *PwC's Annual Corporate Directors Survey.* New York: PwC, October 2020.

Rosenthal, Jeff, Kris Routch, Kelly Monahan, and Meghan Doherty. "The holy grail of effective leadership succession planning: How to overcome the succession planning paradox." *Deloitte Insights.* Hermitage, TN: Deloitte Development LLC, 2018.

Spencer Stuart. 2019 *U. S. Spencer Stuart Board Index.* New York: Spencer Stuart. October, 2019.

Toronto Stock Exchange. *"Where Were the Directors?": Guidelines for Improved Corporate Governance in Canada: Report of the Toronto Stock Exchange Committee on Corporate Governance in Canada.* Toronto: Toronto Stock Exchange. December, 1994.

About the Author

BEVERLY BEHAN has the greatest job in the world.

She's had the privilege of working with Boards of Directors of the S&P1500 and listed companies around the globe for the past 25 years – some of the smartest, nicest, most fascinating and most accomplished people in the world, who keep her at the top of her game. Her clients are typically boards that want to get to the top of *their* game – and stay there.

To date, she's worked with nearly 200 boards, ranging from recent IPOs to the Fortune 500 – from New York and Toronto to Bogota, Kuala Lumpur, and Tel Aviv.

For more than two decades, Bev has not only watched but led much of the evolution of board and director evaluations, dating back to 1996 when she conducted the first director peer review for a major North American bank. In 2001, she incorporated management input into board evaluations for a Fortune 500 publishing company. In 2015, she conducted the first board and director evaluations for one of the largest conglomerates in Southeast Asia – overcoming the concern that individual director evaluations couldn't be effectively adapted to Asian business culture. Over the past decade, she's worked with a number of boards on the development of Board 2.0, an innovation to help boards optimize their composition and manage that transition effectively. And in 2019, she worked with the board of a Fortune 100 company to create what became the New Director 360, an innovation in director evaluations that has both an evaluative and developmental component.

Beverly is the author of *Great Companies Deserve Great Boards* (Palgrave MacMillan, 2011) named **Governance Book of the Year** by *Directors & Boards* magazine and ranked #1 for four weeks on the *Globe & Mail* business best seller list in Canada. A former partner at Mercer Delta in New York and Global Managing Director of the Hay Group's Board Effectiveness practice, Beverly started her own firm, Board Advisor, LLC, in New York in 2009. She can be reached at Beverly.behan@boardadvisor.net.

Why I Started Working with Boards of Directors

About 30 years ago, I took a job with a major Canadian airline – one that no longer exists. It was a prestigious company and its board was populated by marquee-name directors. But it faced major challenges occasioned by the First Gulf War – oil prices had skyrocketed, and people were afraid to travel. Canadian law did not afford our airline the protections of Chapter 11, which our US counterparts were invoking at the time.

To save the company, a group of employees initiated a "wages for stock" arrangement coupled with a joint venture with American Airlines, which needed better access to Asian airports. I worked as part of this team for about two years. We managed to negotiate a deal with all our unions and management employees that involved wage cuts of 5–20%, with these moneys invested in company stock. Morale at the time was nothing short of electric; people who worked for the airline took tremendous pride in their efforts to save it from bankruptcy. The deal raised something in the range of $750 million.

But things soured when the proxy circular revealed that the CEO's salary had been increased, which largely offset his 20% salary cut. In response, the board sent a letter to the homes of company employees, attempting to justify the pay decision. This inflamed the situation and outraged the company's unions. A retired pilot admonished the board at the Annual Shareholder's Meeting – making national headlines. The CEO was replaced – by someone who had run a commercial real estate company in the same Calgary office tower as the airline's headquarters. Within the company, jokes circulated: "Our board members must have run into this guy in the elevator and said, 'Hey, we need a new CEO. You're a CEO. What do you say …?' " The downward spiral continued until the airline was sold to its major rival; tens of thousands lost their jobs. This was my first exposure to how the decisions made by a Board of Directors impacts the "tone at the top" of a company – and many peoples' lives.

I had left the airline shortly after the proxy fiasco and returned to private practice at a Vancouver law firm. There, as a securities and corporate finance attorney, I worked with other boards – nearly all of which were lackluster and characterized by a "country club" mentality. To me, the boardroom was supposed to be where the buck stopped – where smart, capable, experienced people called the question and made a difference. But I saw none of that.

About that time, a Canadian report titled "*Where Were the Directors?*" was issued by the Toronto Stock Exchange.[23] It was a scathing rebuke of the dismal state of corporate governance in Canada. I read it on a Vancouver beach as if it were a racy novel. It confirmed many of the disturbing things I had begun to realize about the way most boards were functioning at that time. As I flipped the pages – almost breathlessly – my friends asked, "What on earth are you reading?" "I'm reading this corporate governance thing!" "Bev," they told me, "you've gotta get a life!" And I realized they were right.

I knew in that moment what I wanted to do: I wanted to work with Boards of Directors – to try to make those boards all that they should be. I've had the privilege of doing that for the past 25 years.

---

23 Committee on Corporate Governance, *"Where Were the directors?": Guidelines for Improved Corporate Governance in Canada.* (Toronto: Toronto Stock Exchange), 1994.

INNOVATIONS IN BOARD-BUILDING:
THE WORKSHOP

The author's on-line workshop features videos on all the key topics and tools covered in this book:

- *The Eight Key Parameters of Board-Building*
- *Tool #1: Redesigned Board Evaluations*
- *Tool #2: Building Board 2.0*
- *Tool #3: Board Composition Benchmarking*
- *Tool #4: Director Evaluations*
- *Tool #5: New Director 360s*

The Workshop also includes our Board-Building Toolkit (eBook) for easy reference.

Available only through our website www.boardadvisor.net – Workshops.

Enter WORKSHOP25 at checkout to receive 25% off - a special discount for those who have already purchased Board and Director Evaluations: Innovations for 21st Century Governance Committees. **If you enjoyed the book, you'll enjoy the Workshop!**

OTHER BOOKS FOR YOUR GOVERNANCE LIBRARY

Just Released

Becoming a Boardroom Star was developed from the author's experience undertaking board and director evaluations at nearly 200 boards over the past 25 years - where more than a thousand board members spoke to her in confidence about the capabilities and contributions of their peers. It's filled with practical insights that can help every director to shine in the boardroom – from new recruits to board leaders – earning the genuine esteem of their peers, the respect of senior management and, most importantly, adding real value for the company they oversee, and its stakeholders.

Coming in October, 2021

Working effectively with the Board of Directors is essential to any CEO's success. It also has implications for the effectiveness of the board, itself. *New CEOs and Boards* offers constructive advice that can help any CEO avoid common pitfalls and get off to a great start in building their board relationship: From analyzing the board you've inherited from your predecessor to building a board-worthy executive team and introducing other initiatives to enhance the way that the board works with management - without a lot of drama. It's an indispensable resource for any new CEO to start their board relationship off on the right foot – and make the most of it throughout their career.

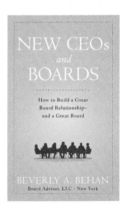

The Classic

Great Companies Deserve Great Boards – the corporate governance classic originally released in 2011 and named Governance Book of the Year in 2012. Initially designed for a CEO audience, this book has nonetheless become essential reading for directors around the world who want to take their boards from good to great and keep great boards vibrant. Look for the Audiobook version in 2021.

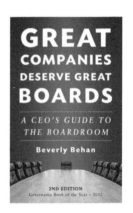

Join our Mailing List!

It's free to sign up. Just visit our website at www.boardadvisor.net.

We'll keep you up to date about book launches, workshops, discounts, complimentary articles, and other items of interest. And don't worry about "email overkill" – we know how annoying that can be. You'll only hear from us when we have something we think will interest you.

Made in the USA
Coppell, TX
06 March 2022